Faith
UnPuzzled

A practical guide to the obtaining of

Faith, Miracles, and Joy!

By:
Carolyn Pearce Ringger

Carolyn P. Ringger

FAITH UNPUZZLED
A practical guide to the obtaining of
Faith, Miracles, and Joy!

This information was researched and organized by
the
Author;
Carolyn Pearce Ringger

Writing Editor: Gertrude O. Smith 1989
2013 Content Layout and Cover Art by:
William J. Burnett

Proof Readers
LaReta Brinkerhoff
Sherry Lincoln
Carolyn P. Ringger

Carolyn P. Ringger

DEDICATION

Faith Unpuzzled is dedicated to
all you dear – brilliant
brothers and sisters
flowing around us.
My desire is that
Faith in Jesus Christ,
may ever increase on the earth.

-- Carolyn Pearce Ringger

Carolyn P. Ringger

CONTENTS

Forward – i

Carolyn P. Ringger

Foreword

The purpose of this lesson material is to share ways to obtain faith, miracles and joy in our lives.

As you see by the "Puzzle Picture" on the cover, there are several major components which will be examined as we work toward a better understanding of what faith is and how it can operate in our lives. Studying each one opens the mind to create a clearer view of the purpose and place of that puzzle part and how they all fit together to help you build a better and more single-minded faith. The final purpose of the whole picture is to help us find Joy through Faith in Jesus Christ.

Use the lessons to unlock faith and its' blessings for yourself and your family. The lesson material is divided into eight parts or "Puzzle Pieces", each one fits together with the next, helping form the whole picture. Take one puzzle piece to study each week. You will note that a comprehensive outline of each section is presented in the appendix of this book. These outlines are useful and can be referred to as a quick reference for lesson or talk preparation, or for a quick review of principles expressed in each chapter. You may even want to go over each outline first, before studying the lesson material of that section. Everything presented in the outline is amplified, expanded upon and clarified in the corresponding chapter in the body of the book.

Lesson concepts are given, first as statements for your use; then presented with scriptures, charts or graphs to help each person understand the concepts better. These are also aids in teaching others.

Many readers have studied and made use of this material, with real results. With their experience comes greater

---

understanding of the Gospel and the joy of following our Savior as their faith in Him increases.

"Men are that they might have joy." --2 Nephi 2: 25

Therefore, the ultimate purpose of these lessons are that we might find joy through understanding the Law of Faith, by which ALL things are possible.

Now is the time for our generation to Awaken to a fuller potential, to learn how to become PURE IN HEART in preparation for the Millennial Reign of Christ upon the earth.

Additional stories and added concepts are found on a 2 CD set which can be obtained, or downloaded to your electronic reader or mp3 player and used along with this book.

Go to:
www.faithunpuzzled.com

Puzzle Piece #1

"Faith Works by Mental Effort"
Joseph Smith

"By Your Positive Inner Self Talk"
Carolyn. P. Ringger

Faith Works by Mental Effort

As you examine the Puzzle Pieces on the front cover, you will note that there are nine pieces that contain words or phrases; each of these puzzle pieces represent important parts of our lives. These parts concern Faith and its role in completing our life, allowing us to solve the puzzles that we experience in this life.

The first puzzle piece is a study on how faith works. As each person becomes a real student, being touched by the Spirit to sincerely "Ask A Question and the Answers Will Be Given To You." You may have thought: "Faith! Yes faith is the first principle of the Gospel, faith in the Lord Jesus Christ." Yet what is that faith? How may I go about acquiring that faith so that I might know how to use it in the right way as the following scripture describes, "Whoso believeth in Christ, doubting nothing, whatsoever he shall ask the Father in the name of Christ it shall be granted him; and this promise is unto all, even unto the ends of the earth." James 1: 5 - 8 teaches us to ask in faith, and if one cannot, he shall receive nothing from the Lord.

We are all familiar with the definition of faith which Paul gives Heb. 11:1 as quoted in the King James Version of the Bible: "Now faith is the substance of things hoped for, the evidence of things not seen." That isn't really very clear. The wording as given in the Inspired Version of the Bible, through Joseph Smith, clarifies this somewhat, as does the definition of faith given in Alma 32:21 in the Book of Mormon.

The Inspired Version, JST (Joseph Smith Translation) quotes it as follows:	"Now faith is the assurance of things hoped for, the proof of things not seen."
Alma describes faith as follows in Alma 32:21:	"faith is not to have a perfect knowledge of things; therefore, if ye have faith ye hope for things which are not seen, which are true."

The following chart shows what I am finally seeing, as the meaning of *Faith:*

Faith = You Believe In Jesus Christ =

Your Positive Inner Self-Talk About Christ =

You Doubt Not that He Lives as our Resurrected Savior and King and That
He Can Do All Things =

Stop being Double Minded and Become SINGLE-MINDED -*James:2-8*

1. Jesus Christ Lives	1. When you know that Jesus Christ lives and you Doubt Him Not, you have *Faith in Him*! -- *Mosiah 9:18-27*
2. He is Pure In Heart	2. When you repent and are **watching over your thoughts,** you become more and more Pure in Heart. Your inner vessel is cleansing each day, and you have the power to ask and receive – *Mosiah 4:30, 1 John 3:2-3, D&C 46:30.*
3. He Can Do All Things	3. You can connect your Hopes and Desires with **His Power** by being Single Minded. You then have Faith. **Miracles are real today by Faith in Jesus Christ.** – *Moroni 7:20-30 -- Mosiah 24:10-17 – Mormon 9:18-21.*

You Can Become Of One Mind And One Heart With The Lord, or Pure in
Your Thoughts.

"That they all may be one; as thou, Father, art in me,
and I in thee, that they also may be one in us:"
– St. John 17:21

As you grow in the reality that Jesus Christ lives, you doubt Him not, then you will grow in understanding, and have more faith. It is a widening and enlarging circle. Faith in Christ begets more understanding and understanding begets more faith and miracles in your life today.

Since our desire is to find out how **Faith in Jesus Christ** works, and how to put it into our lives, let us go to the next step and discover who we are.

First come to know that:

We are spirit intelligence and intelligences think

Do you notice how your spirit intelligence
is always thinking inside your body?

As spirit intelligence, you will be with yourself
for eternity.

Another realization is:

"To think takes mental effort."

What is Thinking?

~Thinking is part of your inner self talk and the Prophet Joseph Smith explained that:

~"Faith works by your mental effort."
-- *Lectures on Faith,* p. 61 #3, by Joseph Smith

~Therefore <u>Could</u> Faith Be <u>Connected</u> <u>To</u> Your
Positive Inner Self-Talk?

To recap then:

- You are spirit intelligence
- Spirit intelligences think
- As spirit intelligences we will be with ourselves for eternity – connected with our Resurrected body

Therefore each of us needs to desire to be happy within ourselves.

Each person can learn:
- How to love yourself and others
- How to have faith in yourself and Jesus Christ
- How to become master of yourself through Positive Inner-Self Talk

You are not your body.
You are not your brain.
You are Spirit Intelligence, you are the thought monitor, the thought chooser, the thought maker or thought creator.

How Do You Work By Faith?

Joseph Smith offers an explanation to this question. I first came across this concept in the book by Paul H. Dunn, *I Challenge You, I Promise You,* Vol. II page 20: "Faith works by mental effort." Two Elders of the Arizona Tempe Mission shared with me the original material as found in *Lectures on Faith.* The Prophet Joseph Smith tells us:

Let us here offer some explanation in relation to faith, that our meaning may be clearly comprehended. We ask, then, what are we to understand by a man's working by faith? We answer – we understand that when a man works by faith he works by mental exertion instead of physical force. It is by words, instead of exerting his physical powers, with which every being works when he works by faith. –*Lectures on Faith,* page 61 #3, by Joseph Smith

If faith works by your mental effort, and the tools used are thoughts, then let us learn more about where your thoughts come from. To begin, let me share an idea from the book, *Life After Life,* by Dr. Raymond Moody. The following is an account of a woman who died on the operating table, and returned to life. She shares:

> I was more conscious of my mind at the time than of that physical body. The mind [or thought] was the most important part, instead of the shape of the body. And before, all my life, it had been exactly reversed. The body was my main interest and what was going on in my mind, well, it was just going on, and that's all. But after this happened, my mind [thought] was the main point of attraction, and the body was second – it was only something to encase my mind... -- Life After Life, page 91, by Dr. Raymond Moody

This woman realized that her *thoughts* stayed with her when she was away from her body and brain. She was still alive, thinking!

Here is another experience taken from the book *Return From Tomorrow* by Dr. George Ritchie, which opened my mind's eye about death. Visualize with me this unique situation as you read Dr. Ritchie's own experience. When he realized he had lost his solidness, his body, so that mortals were not aware of his presence and could not respond, he thought, "Am I dead?" Says he:

> But I wasn't dead! How could I be dead and still be awake? Thinking. Experiencing. Death was different. Death was – I didn't know. Blanking out. Nothingness. [But] I was wide awake, only without a physical body to function in. – *Return From Tomorrow*, pages 47-48, by Dr. George Ritchie

Dr. Ritchie realized he was dead, yet still alive within his spirit and was talking, thinking and trying to communicate with mortals.

The following story again reveals to us the reality of our spirit intelligence self.

The following incident happened in the life of Bishop and Sister John J. Wells, a former member of the Presiding Bishopric. The story illustrates how we may receive communication from those who have passed on, and how we must be responsive to the whisperings of other Spirit souls who are unseen to our mortal eyes yet are still around us.

Bishop and Sister Wells had a son who was killed in a railroad accident in Emigration Canyon, east of Salt Lake

City. He had been run over by a freight car. Sister Wells received no comfort after the funeral, and she mourned for their son.

Then one day, soon after the funeral, as she was laying on her bed in a state of great sorrow, their son appeared to her. He told her, "Mother, don't mourn. Don't cry. I am all right." Then he told her how the accident had occurred. He then told her that he had tried to make contact with his father as soon as he realized he was in another sphere. He had been unable to do so, however, because his father had been so occupied [in his thoughts] with the affairs of his work. And so he had been unable to get through to him. The young man then said, "Tell Father all is well with me, and I want you not to mourn anymore."

President David O. McKay and President Harold B. Lee often used this story as an illustration in their talks, to point out the necessity of being receptive to the Spirit and to take time to ponder and meditate each day so that we can hear when information needs to reach us. –*Come Unto Christ,* p. 18, by President Ezra Taft Benson.

These experiences have taught me that if I were to die right now, I would realize immediately that I am not this body and I am not this brain. I am Spirit Intelligence living inside of a body (The Lord's word is "Temple") and it can be influenced for good or evil because both good and evil come into our mind as thoughts.

What if someone decided he could not stand living any longer? He hates the person he is; he hates life and wants to commit suicide. The first thing he would realize after committing the death-causing act is that his body is dead but his spirit, the thinking part of him is still alive, thinking and experiencing. You cannot get rid of yourself through the death of your body.

Your Thinking Intelligence is the real part. Your body is merely the temple to hold your spirit. Each of us need to learn to love ourselves, as the Savior said. Since I will be around me for eternity, I need to learn how to become my own best friend and learn how to follow the Spirit of Light and Truth.

Now is the time for each of us to start liking-loving ourselves. We can do this by finding out how we can become the person we desire to become. You are one of the most important people You will ever know, for only You can purify your thoughts (Your Heart) through your own self-talk. Only You can get You to follow our Savior, Jesus Christ.

The way is to come unto Him through the ordinances of the Gospel. Each of us must repent, be baptized by one having the authority and learn ways of becoming pure in heart. Then, when the Savior arrives we will be able to see him, for it is the "Pure In Heart Shall See God". Oh, do you see that we can begin to accomplish this by watching over our thoughts, our real self, starting now?

We really are Spirit Intelligence – the thinking part of us. We are not this body. We are not our brain within. We are Spirit Intelligence. But, since thoughts are the real and creative part of our "Self", let us go one step further by understanding more about our brain and how it works with the thoughts created by our "Thought Creating" intelligence.

Understanding the brain and how it works.

The brain is not your intelligence; it is merely a servo-mechanism – a computer-like system, given us by our Heavenly Father to help us think and act. It does the processing, sorting, and filing of the thoughts and information given. It is a very highly sophisticated computer which operates at our command. It accepts what you give it and the subconscious sorts and files away that material. We speak of right-brain learning, which is related to the creative side of our brain, and of left-brain learning, which handles the mathematical and precision aspects of learning. There is also the conscious and subconscious level of the mind. The conscious level does the recording; the subconscious, the sorting and filing and storing.

But the brain is not our intelligence. Our Spirit Intelligence is the real "I." It is the Spirit Intelligence which we interact with to form the identity of who we really are.

It was through the study of the brain and how it operates that I came to better understand how the laws of Faith work. I discovered that by programming new thoughts into my brain-servant, I could alter my self-image and thereby alter my life. My thoughts are live electrical energy which I create by my mental effort or my Inner Self-Talk. I can develop Faith through my Positive Inner Self-Talk, created by my spirit intelligence, which is the *real* me.

Since the brain is a servo-mechanism, each of us needs to understand how it operates in order to make the best use of it. And, as we control our thoughts and physical actions better, we indeed become masters of our self, and more fully able to choose to follow The Light of Christ into his presence.

This knowledge about the brain has been a missing link, one we have not understood until now. The brain operates as a computer at our command. Thought controls the flesh and we control the thoughts and through it we learn to become masters of ourselves.

We as humans have not understood this. This is part of the reason why it is so hard for us sometimes to know how to gain control of ourselves. The Lord has given us information about this in the scriptures, but somehow we did not make the connection on how to use it. When we understand the brain and how to properly "program it", we are in a much better position to be in control of the Spirit Intelligence called "I", and to be master of this temple which we call our body.

The existence of the conscious mind is an accepted medical fact. Think of the subconscious mind as a computer. As a result, all thoughts and actions actually program the subconscious mind. The data is all placed in your mind's storage banks, which according to tape #1 in The Neuropsychology of Achievement by Syber Vision, contains over 200 billion brain cells, the eyes being a part of that cell count. If you think more negative thoughts than positive, you are programming yourself an unhappy life.

If you are not the person you want to be, what are you doing to become that person? Are you feeding proper data into your mental computer? For you must remember, it will give back only what you have placed there. As a man soweth so shall he reap. Your thoughts are the seeds which are sown and you will harvest what you sow.

The negative input from the world can affect your faith.

Your thoughts are an extension of your faith "to think takes mental effort"

Positive Thought Is Positive Faith. Negative Thought Is Negative Faith.

Thoughts are electrical energy and trigger the brain to create chemicals. – Candice Perk Ph.D
In her book Molecules of Emotion

That energy attracts you to whatever you think about the most, just as surely as a magnet is pulled to metal. – Sterling W. Sill

As a man thinketh in his heart [or thoughts], so is he." --Proverbs 23:7

How Does The Brain Operate?

Three figures will help give a much clearer understanding of how the brain functions, and how the conscious and subconscious mind operate. Figure 1 shows a sketch of the brain shape and shows how the eye is connected directly to the brain stem as a living camera, your personal Video Camera. Figure 2 shows sleeping and waking brain wave patterns. Figure 3 illustrates the Beta and Alpha brain wave pattern concept.

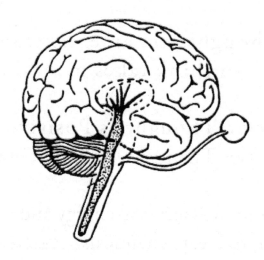

FIGURE 1. The Eye Is Directly Connected To The Human Brain

Notice that the eye is an actual extension of the brain and acts as a camera lens to record what you see, i.e. it is your video camera. We have a type of photographic memory ability.

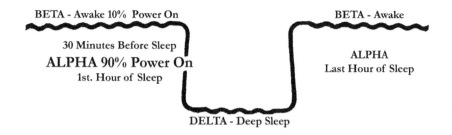

FIGURE 2. Thought Power Increases

When You Relax And Reach The Alpha State

Note, it is the Alpha level which is the most important. Your brain is on Record when in Alpha, with 90% of your power in use. You are in Alpha when you are relaxed as you study, as you think or meditate, ponder and pray. You are there 30 minutes before sleep, plus the first and last hour of sleep. When you are in the Alpha brain wave state, your subconscious mind accepts your *self-talk* as internal *Life-Directing* instruction most readily. The brain is the computer-servant and you are the programmer.

The Beta Level is when you are awake and alert, and it would be logical that most of our learning would occur at this level. Yet, interestingly enough it is the Alpha or relaxed level where most learning occurs.

What significance does this have as far as our learning and use of time are concerned? Consider again, some of the times when your brain is at the Alpha Level:

- 30 minutes before sleep, and the first and last hour of sleep.
- When you relax in the daytime to read and ponder or meditate.
- When you are watching TV.
- When you are at the movies.
- When you deliberately relax just before studying or taking an exam.
- Listening to the radio or entertainment (good, bad or indifferent).

Today, many Doctors teach Biofeedback principles to help their patients control pain as a result of personal injury. In the area of helping cancer patients, some doctors teach how to Mentally Visualize an attacking force like "Pac-Man" images, which help eat up the cancer cells. The reports show that when a patient does this, the body's ability to fight the malignancy increases noticeably. The patient learns how to tune into their INNER SELF-TALK, to communicate with the body at the brain's Alpha level. They learn to Think instructive thoughts when they are in the relaxed Alpha state.

Thoughts, being electrical impulses, flow to the brain and then to the nervous system. The patient becomes the person in charge of his or her own body instead of the pain being in charge. By using thoughts as instructions to their cells, the patients lie down and does slow, deep breathing in order to relax the body. This causes the brain waves to shift into the Alpha Level. The patient mentally Talks to himself and instructs the body to stop the pain.

Harvey and Marilyn Diamond explain in their book, *Fit For Life,* that we can talk to the intelligence in the cells of our body:

Every cell in your body is teeming with life and possesses its own intelligence. Each cell is like a soldier in the army, awaiting its instructions. We are constantly sending messages or commands to our cells, and those commands are carried out diligently. What I'm suggesting is that we can consciously direct our cells to do what we want them to do. The body will bring about whatever result the conscious mind desires. The mind is continuously assessing the body's condition and forming images in line with what it believes to be true. We can literally change our bodies by changing the way we think about them, even in the face of data or evidence that conflicts. –p. 92-93, *Fit For Life,* by Harvey and Marilyn Diamond

Alpha level programming works in the same way. Each of us can learn to relax our body so that our brain wave can shift into Alpha, giving us 90% of our mental power. One idea would be to write your own affirmation – record it in your own voice, then listen to your self made recording to pattern your thoughts. You can read your goals or Righteous Desires to give your Servo-Mechanism, your brain computer, your instructions telling it how you desire your Servant to function. Your initial thoughts create an electromagnetic force field. This process leads you to be attracted to subsequent thoughts. Your job is to stay single-minded so you can receive your spiritual creation. You create your future by what you think about today. You first create tomorrow spiritually before it is created physically. "As a man soweth, so shall he reap." That which you sow is your Thoughts. Thoughts then, are seeds; they are the tools used to create your reality.

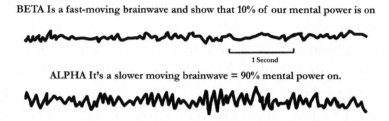

BETA Is a fast-moving brainwave and show that 10% of our mental power is on

1 Second

ALPHA It's a slower moving brainwave = 90% mental power on.

Subconscious programming can be used to bless or destroy men and nations.

As I have researched this material on the brain to help me learn how to improve my own self-image and increase my Joy for life, another realization was presented to my mind by the spirit of truth. Others have taken these facts on how to affect the subconscious mind and are using them to promote immorality and more filthy language in our land. The movies, television, and internet do affect us, our families and our nation. I have heard young mothers use curse-words that we would not allow our children to use a generation ago. Men act as if using curse-words is okay in front of me, and I am insulted. We have the right to not hear the filth of the world!

Dr. Dean Black of the BioResearch Foundation, explains on his tapes, *Meeting Life's Challenges*, that we are what is called an open system. This, he explains, means that everything we see or hear goes into our mental system and influences us. So, the things that we expose ourselves to are the things which go into our storage banks and influence how we think and feel. We are influenced by Satellite, Cable TV and movies. Satan knows this. He knows that one of the best and most effective ways to influence a whole nation is through its entertainment.

As the level of public entertainment crumbles, the level of our private morals will crumble as well unless we keep ourselves aware and are very careful. The spoiler knows how to subconsciously program a whole nation to accept a gradually deteriorating standard. And the movie industry actually charges us to go into their deprogramming booths (movie theaters), and the people say, "We can't help it if the movies show nudity or use filthy language. Besides, this isn't influencing me anyway." We are an open system and we have been fooled. (2 Ne. 28:20-22). Movie scripts are written. The situations in movies do not just happen. They are written, practiced and performed. The words, the salaciousness, the nudity, filth, and immorality etc. have been designed to weaken mankind and to lead mankind away from their potential.

In a similar vein, as I have studied truths in systems of government, I have come to know the greatness of our constitutional system. As I read the book, *The Real Thomas Jefferson,* by Allison, Maxfield, Cook and Skousen, I realized that our country has always had an enemy to our constitutional system. Even George Washington and Thomas Jefferson had to deal with men who wanted to change the government in ways that could prove destructive.

I have taken time to study the Constitution. I have

researched how we could solve our nation's problems. I have concluded that by returning to the original Constitutional wording, and the Founding Fathers' real intent we can restore founding freedoms. I have also studied the intent of the negative forces and how they say they will bring our nation down. The negative forces are using the same knowledge on how the brain functions, and that people can be programmed. Their purpose, though, is to destroy others and by this means to accomplish their own wicked ends.

Let me quote but a few of the 45 goals which the enemy of all has declared to be part of their plan to destroy this and other nations. The following material was compiled by the FBI in 1958.

> #24. Eliminate all laws governing obscenity by calling them "censorship" and a violation of free speech and free press.

> #25. Break down cultural standards of morality by promoting pornography and obscenity in books, magazines, motion pictures, radio and TV [and Internet].

> #26. Present homosexuality, degeneracy and promiscuity as "normal, natural, [and] healthy."

> #27. Infiltrate the churches and replace revealed religion with "social" religion. Discredit the Bible and emphasize the need for intellectual maturity which does not need a "religious crutch."

#28. Eliminate prayer or any phase of religious expression in the schools on the ground that it violates the principle of "separation of church and state." [Our Constitution states that we shall have no state church. In Sweden, the state church – or the church that is supported by their government is the Lutheran church. I understand that everyone pays the tax to the state church, whether you are Lutheran or not. We do not have a church to which our republic pays a tax. We have freedom of religion. It does not say we should separate morals or religious influences from our government.]

#29. Discredit the American Constitution by calling it inadequate, old-fashioned, out of step...

#30. Discredit the American Founding Fathers. (Lies can be found in some textbooks today.)

#40. Discredit the family as an institution. Encourage promiscuity and easy divorce.
--*The Naked Communist*, by W. Cleon Skousen, p. 260-62. Copyright 1958, by Ensign Pub. Co.

John Adams explained: "Our Constitution was made only for a moral and religious people. It is wholly inadequate to the government of any other." --John Adams, The Changing Political Thought of John R. Howe. (Princeton, N.J.: Princeton University Press, 1966), p. 189.

Benjamin Franklin said: "Only a virtuous people are capable of freedom. As nations become corrupt and vicious, they have more need of masters." --Albert Henry Smyth, Ed., The Writings of Benjamin Franklin, 10 vols. (New York Macmillan Co., 1905-7), 9:569.

This being true, then how could you destroy the United States of America? Yes, through Immorality, the avenue our enemies are using. The enemies are from without and also within. America's Trojan Horse is Immorality. We can choose to awaken and to Repent, little by little until we become People that are Pure in Heart.

Now we will return back to the Scriptures to understand what the Lord desires for us to learn about the words heart, mind, and brain.

What is the difference in the meaning between the words heart, mind, and brain?

The words heart, mind, and brain are sometimes used interchangeably. Or the same words may be used to denote different meanings. The scriptures also use the words **Heart** and **Mind** interchangeably. So this can cause, and often has caused a great deal of confusion. What does the Lord mean when he speaks of our **Heart** and our **Mind**? Let us turn to the scriptures to see if we can gain a better understanding of these terms, how they are being used, and what they mean.

Do you think with your heart in your chest or with your heart in your mind?

In order to answer this question let us consider and see how the word Heart is used in the scriptures. Some words appear to be like secret code. In order to understand the code, we need to search out the real word meanings, so that our minds can comprehend what we have read.

I have realized that if I substitute the word Heart with the word Thoughts or Mind, that I have greater understanding of what I am reading. Let us start out with the following three scriptures:

- D&C 8:2-4
- D&C 100:5
- Alma 16:16

I will tell you in your mind and in your heart.
2. Yea, behold, I will tell you in your mind and in your heart, by the Holy Ghost, which shall come upon you and which shall dwell in your heart.

3. Now, behold, this is the spirit of revelation; behold, this is the spirit by which Moses brought the children of Israel through the Red Sea on dry ground.

4. Therefore this is thy gift; apply unto it, and blessed art thou, ... -- D&C 8:2-4

Thoughts I shall put into your heart.
5. Therefore, verily I say unto you, lift up your voices unto this people; speak the thoughts that I shall put into your hearts, and you shall not be confounded before men. -- D&C 100:5

Prepare the minds or hearts.

> 16. And there was no inequality among them; the Lord did pour out his Spirit on all the face of the land to prepare the minds of the children of men, or to prepare their hearts to receive the word which should be taught among them at the time of his coming. -- Alma 16:16

Notice how Alma uses the words mind and hearts interchangeably

Thoughts stimulate emotions. Have some fun by returning to the above quotes and substitute the word heart for thoughts.

Thoughts stimulate emotions in your body, which affect your actions. When you "Feel" emotion, how do you describe where you "FEEL" it? You say that you "Feel" it in your "Heart." This word "Heart" describes the whole experience: where you receive positive or enlightening thoughts from the Lord in your mind, then you start to "Feel" His influence, and you say you "Feel" it in your "Heart", when in fact I think that it is coming into your mind as impressions and thoughts which have triggered the body's emotions.

We each need to improve our spiritual listening skills to be able to hear the whisperings of the Spirit of the Lord within each of us. Each of us is a live receiving set. Thoughts are electrical energy, which you pick up within your mind.

Imagine that there are two spiritual Internet Servers, E-mailing or Energy-mailing "Ideas" into your mind. One is from the Lord and the other from the Satan. We need to recognize the spiritual beginnings of MANY of our thoughts. We receive more than we know.

We can learn to "Feel" when a thing is right or "Feel" when it is wrong by tuning into our emotional responses, our feeling center.

In addition to the scriptures previously cited, a number of quotations from our modern prophets and general Church authorities help us get a clearer picture of how the Lord is speaking to us, and how we receive His promptings and directions.

Consider what the Prophet Joseph Smith had to say on the subject. Said he:

> All things whatsoever God in his infinite wisdom has seen fit and proper to reveal to us, while we are dwelling in mortality, in regard to our mortal bodies, are revealed to us in the abstract, and independent of affinity of this mortal tabernacle, but are revealed to our spirits precisely as though we had no bodies at all. - - Teachings of the Prophet Joseph Smith, p. 355.

Now let us examine a quote which was taken from the Church News, Feb. 4, 1989, p. 5

Promise Follows Prayerful Study

If you prayerfully study and ponder the words in the Doctrine and Covenants, you have the promise of hearing the voice of the Lord. (See D&C 18:33-36.) That voice may not be an audible expression that resonates off your ear drum, but more important, it will come into your mind and your heart, leaving an indelible impression of far more lasting significance and power. (See D&C 8:2-3.) -Hoyt Brewster Jr., director of Melchizedek Priesthood Department

Opposition in All Things
But because we have opposition in all things know that a similar system of communication is also used by the negative element in our universe, controlled by Satan

You are a Spiritual Receiving Set...

... You Receive Thoughts or Impressions
... Into Your Heart – Your Mind!

You are a live receiving set. You can receive your promptings from God, or you can attune yourself to the negative whisperings of Satan. Thoughts create emotions in your body which affect your actions.

Your Thoughts are Live Electrical Energy!

Imagine two internet servers, that are emailing thoughts or speaking into your mind, one from the Lord, the other from Satan. You need to recognize the spiritual beginnings of your thoughts.

We receive more than we know. We can learn to feel when a thing is right, or feel when it is wrong, by tuning into our emotional responses. This can develop into a spiritual gift – the gift of discernment.

The scriptures bear this out in many places.

Let us go to D&C 10:10, 13, to see what the Lord has to say about spiritual communication.

This example is about Joseph Smith finally giving in to Martin Harris to allow him to show the book of Mormon manuscript to his wife. The translation was lost. Joseph's direction was not to lend it out. Because he went against that inspiration Satan then plotted to rewrite parts of the manuscript to discredit Joseph's work of translation.

Satan hath put it into their hearts.
10. And, behold, Satan hath put it into their hearts to alter the words which you have caused to be written, or which you have translated, which have gone out of your hands.

13. For he hath put into their hearts to do this, that by lying they may say they have caught you in the words which you have pretended to translate.
-- D&C 10:10, 13

How can you distinguish between the two "Internet Servers"?

Realize that your Heavenly Father always works by positive, pure, and enlightening thoughts.

Good comes from God.
17. Every good gift and every perfect gift is from above, and cometh down from the father of lights, with whom is no variableness, neither shadow of turning. -- James 1:17

12. Wherefore, all things which are good cometh of god; and that which is evil cometh of the devil; for the devil is an enemy unto God, and fighteth against him continually, and inviteth and enticeth to sin, and to do that which is evil continually. -- Moroni 7:12

Our Heavenly Father does not tempt us with evil.

Your trials and temptations come into your life through your own weaknesses.

The evil one tempts you wherever you are weak.
We are in an Earth school, or situation. Each day this gives us an opportunity to become a real-life student, one who can choose to overcome each weakness and transform it into strength.

Here is what our Heavenly Father teaches us.

Let no man say, I am tempted of God

12. Blessed is the man that endureth temptation: for when he is tried, he shall receive the crown of life, which the Lord hath promised to them that love him.

13. Let no man say when he is tempted, I am tempted of God: for God cannot be tempted with evil, neither tempteth he any man:

14. But every man is tempted, when he is drawn away of his own lust *[weaknesses]*, and enticed. -- James 1: 12-14

The devil works by putting negative, doubting, evil, or fearful thoughts into your mind.

His goal is to "spoil" your life.
The word devil in Hebrew means "Spoiler"
In Greek his name means slanderer demon or adversary.

Description as found in the LDS Bible dictionary Page 656.

Devil – The English word devil in the KJV is used to represent several different words in Greek, i.e., slanderer, demon, and adversary, and Hebrew, i.e., spoiler. The devil is the enemy of righteousness and of those who seek to do the will of God. Satan as a spirit son of God, rebelled in the pre-mortal life, at which time he persuaded a third of the host of heaven to rebel with him, in opposition to the plan of salvation championed by Jehovah (Jesus Christ). "Thus came the devil and his angels!" (D&C 29:37). They were cast out of heaven, and were denied the experience of mortal bodies and earth life. ...One of the major techniques of the devil is to cause human beings to think they are following God's ways, when in reality they are being deceived by the devil to follow other paths. ...Protection against the influence of the devil is found by obedience to the commandments and laws of the gospel of Jesus Christ.

The term "SPOILER" describes him well!

Assignments

1. Watch over your THOUGHTS and replace any Negative thought with new Positive thoughts. Just mentally say – "I delete that thought – like deleting a bad email – you are not a bad person because you have a bad thought. A bad thought is equal to a bad email or an evil email. Just as we delete bad emails or spam we need to take our mental cursor and delete the bad thought. We need to put it in the trash, like we would on a computer, and then delete it.

2. Read the book *Return From Tomorrow*, by Dr. George Ritchie to be able to see beyond your mortal eyes.

3. Purchase the CD by Dr. Charles Beckert: *What Husbands Wish Their Wives Knew about Men*, and the CD

(currently out of production but is occasionally found on eBay or Amazon.)

The Atonement: A Personal Search for the Meaning of the Atonemen, by Dr. W. Cleon Skousen.

4. As you **Pray**, say: "I ask for further **Light and Knowledge** on **How The Law Of Faith Works**."

5. Highlight the following words in your scriptures: FAITH, HOPE, DESIRE, HEART, THOUGHTS, MIND, SINGLE-MINDED, DOUBLE-MINDED, BELIEF, UNBELIEF, ASK, PRAY, REPENT, and DOUBT NOT. DO you see what the Lord is telling us regarding **The Law of Faith** and how it works to discern and delete an evil thought.

Have fun!

PUZZLE PIECE #2
What Are My Hopes, Desires or Goals?

Carolyn P. Ringger

36

Hopes Desires or Goals

What Are My Hopes, Desires, and Goals?

How Do You Use Your Positive Mental Effort To Make Faith Work For You?

Faith is a mental process and the scriptures have a great deal to say about it.

Let us Learn more about Faith from Moroni 7.

Concerning faith, hope and charity

And now I, Moroni, write a few of the words of my father Mormon, which he spake concerning faith, hope, and charity; ... -- Moroni 7:1

Lay hold on every good thing.

20. And now, my brethren, how is it possible that ye can lay hold upon every good thing?

21. And now I come to that faith, of which I said I would speak; and I will tell you the way whereby ye may lay hold on every good thing. -- Moroni 7:20-21

To have faith ye must have hope

40. And again, my beloved brethren, I would speak unto you concerning hope. How is it that ye can attain unto faith, save ye shall have hope?
-- Moroni 7:40

Faith defined

Now faith is the substance of things hoped for, the evidence of things not seen. -- Hebrews 11:1

The Joseph Smith translation clarifies this passage

Now faith is the assurance of things hoped for, the proof of things not seen. -- Hebrews 11:1 (JST)

Does this not give a clearer understanding of the meaning and process of faith?

To Hope Takes "Mental Effort"
Let us say that Faith Means for You to:
"Think" Positive Thoughts
about Your Hopes
Doesn't this take Mental Effort?

To repeat then, he is saying:
Ask Of God, Nothing Wavering

> 2. My brethren, count it all joy when ye fall into divers temptations.

> 3. Knowing this, that the trying of your faith worketh patience.

> 4. But let patience have her perfect work, that ye may be perfect and entire, wanting nothing.

> 5. If any of you lack wisdom, let him ask of God, that giveth to all men liberally, and upbraideth not; and it shall be given him.

> 6. But let him ask in faith, [Positive Thoughts] nothing wavering, [No Negative Thoughts]. For he that wavereth is like a wave of the sea driven with the wind and tossed.

> 7. For let not that man think that he shall receive anything of the Lord.

8. A double minded man is unstable in all his ways.
-- James 1:2-8

- You must ask in faith, nothing wavering (or no negative thoughts).
- He that wavereth shall not receive anything from the Lord.
- A double-minded man is unstable in all his ways for his thought and energy are going in two different directions.
- But when he is single-minded his thoughts and energy are focused, directed, and powerful.

Prayer is your thought, and thought is electrical energy. We humans use electrical energy for telephone, radio, and TV and Internet to transmit our messages. But the Eternal Beings have a better system than telephones or e-mail to hear us and return the calls or e-mail. They communicate with us by thoughts, ideas, dreams, and impressions. And your thoughts are likewise communicated to them as a **Prayer in the Heart** (Mosiah 24:10-17). You communicate your faith, hopes and desires through your thoughts and prayers and your positive Self-Talk. Through this means you ask those unseen beings to help you with your hopes and desires (which are also unseen by you) = to hope for things not seen. Hebrews 11:1

A Double-Minded person can receive nothing from the Lord because he is just not "tuned in" so he can receive from the Lord. His thoughts, (therefore Faith) are scattered, negative, and weak.

What then can a Single-Minded person do? Through his faith and through the Power of God he can do all things. Like the people of the City of Enoch, who were of one mind and one heart, (they were pure in heart – or thought and actions), that person would be able to receive the spirit and power of the Lord, to receive the righteous desires of their "Heart."

Let us discuss further:

- What does it mean to be double-minded?
- It means you have allowed negative, doubting, evil or fearful thoughts to enter into your mind through your ungaurded thoughts, so you are led in two directions at once.

Then What Does It Take To Stop
Negative, Doubting, Evil, or Fearful Thoughts?

It Takes Your Mental Effort or FAITH

With Your Inner Self-Talk, Mentally Say: "I Erase that thought." (See p. 90)

This is like the scripture principle: "Get Thee Behind Me Satan!"

Now we are learning to be Single Minded.

Always remember that:
> To Erase A Negative Thought
> Just Takes Your Mental Effort, or Your Faith!

You achieve this through:
> Your positive inner self-talk

- Repeat in your mind these words: "I know that Jesus Christ Lives and I Doubt Him Not. I ask for further light and knowledge, wilt thou teach me what I need to know or do. Then listen and do what you are taught that which is positive, pure and enlightening.
- Mentally repeat the above, until all doubts are cleared from your mind.

Agree Technique

Here is a technique which allows you to agree with a negative thought and remain in control.

> 25. **Agree with thine adversary quickly, whiles thou art in the way with him;** lest at any time the adversary deliver thee to the judge, and the judge deliver thee to the officer, and thou be cast into prison. -- Matt. 5:25

> 25. **Agree with thine adversary quickly while thou art in the way with him,** lest at any time he shall get thee, and thou shalt be cast into prison. -- 3 Nephi 12:25

We are learning that the "Spoiler" approaches each of us through our thoughts. I have come to realize that the prison in which we often find ourselves is due to the feeling of disappointment in our selves. Allowing the negative thoughts to stay and haunt you can cause depression. Remember that the negative thought triggers creation of depressant molecules. Your brain is a chemical factory (Dr. Candace Pert). The negative spirit speaks to your spirit. He whispers in your ear and you hear it in your mind (most often in your own tone of voice) as described in 2 Nephi 28:22 "and thus he whispereth in their ears." He takes a situation where you are weak and then tells you negative thoughts about yourself to make you doubt and fear, that you might be miserable, even as he is miserable.

Situation #1

Let us suppose that you had a bad morning with your family and you yelled at your children. The spoiler will remind you of your negative action and rub your nose in it, telling you that 'You' are not a good parent because 'You' yelled at your children. (Think up your own last negative situation. See the realness of this idea in your own life.)

First the evil hosts will tell you that: "You are a bad parent because you yelled at your kids." The spoiler will add to the above accusation, with his own insidious reasoning. "Since **you** are a bad parent, why don't **you** leave?" or "Wouldn't it be better for **you** to go out to work since **you** do not enjoy being with your children" or anything else, and make it go from bad to worse? He wants **you** to think that **you** are not good enough just because you made an uncontrolled choice. You chose to yell at your children.

Do not let the negative thoughts haunt you until you feel depressed within. That is what the spoiler's team wants you to do. There are many voices trying to get your attention. You can feel like a prisoner in your own body.

Instead, the best way to handle this situation is to "Agree with thine adversary quickly". The way I do it is <u>first</u> to agree with some part that has truth to it. (A Negative Truth Is Still A Negative!) I say: "I agree. I did yell at my children." (You have just taken away the argument.)

Next: I ask the Lord to forgive me. Then I ask others to forgive me, those whom the Spirit impresses upon my mind to go to. Then I choose to forgive myself. Use the Gospel for your *Shield of Faith* to assault the negative thoughts which try to make you believe that you are of no worth due to your choices. Each of us can choose again until it is Love we choose Next, I ask to receive Light and Knowledge into my mind, to teach me how I can choose better. I listen for the inspiration, which teaches me how to improve myself. Then, I work to choose positive thoughts that come to me, pressing itself upon my mind. Joseph Smith shares this type of concept in D & C 128:1. "I now resume the subject of baptism for the dead, as that subject seems to occupy my mind, and impress itself upon my feelings the strongest ."

I tell the spoiling element that I love them. (These spirit beings cannot increase in power when you throw love at them.) I tell them that they are a part of the large spiritual family, but that I do not agree with the thoughts they are telling me.

Then the last command I give to the negative thoughts is that they must leave, for I have moral agency, and I do not choose to listen to their thoughts any more. Then I mentally request, through my self-talk, for angels, whom I cannot see, to come and protect me from the negative forces, which I cannot see. I also make a request for a spiritual Shield to cover me like a glass dome, and it is so. I ask for the shield to become thicker when I need more help. The evil thoughts cannot get through. I am humbly amazed at how much power we can develop by our faith. I am aware of when the evil thoughts cease. I can feel the inner peace arrive, and the frustration, evil thoughts, or fear dissipates.

Situation #2

The temptation of the "natural man" is something which the male gender learns to accept. Our brothers are created to be visually stimulated. The spoiler places thoughts about women into a man's mind. For instance, the spoiler can send suggestive thoughts about how shapely the woman is, then builds upon those thoughts, to whatever extent the boy or man will allow. Then he will plant more and more thoughts of impurity in that person's mind until soon the individual is committing adultery with her in his heart (or thoughts). This then can lead to the actual step of that person committing the act. Because the natural response of the male body is hardwired or automatically stimulated visually, his male motor can just turn on. This is one of the big reasons our brothers - males - can be attracted to pornography. Staying away from pornography takes mental effort and faith to help him through.

Women also can be haunted by this problem, if they are willing to listen to the negative, insidious reasoning which the spoiler sends out to destroy all who will listen. All this involves a mental battle, unseen by others, which continues until the fruits of evil show. Or, in contrast, by casting off the evil thoughts, the person reaps the fruits of good by following the **Light of Christ.**

Too many men and women are acting like robots today. We are allowing ourselves to react to the thoughts which are placed in our minds by the adversary. We all must realize that the spoiler is behind negative, doubting, evil or unjustified fearful thoughts. The Natural Man, the Natural Woman, and the Natural Older Child/Teenager might become an enemy to God. Teenagers, men, and women all are sons and daughters of God, and must become mentally-morally clean in order to have the protective hand of God upon them. **We can become pure in heart today and tomorrow by awakening to our power of choice and our power to delete each negative thought.**

The Savior has said:

27. Behold, it is written by them of old time, that thou shalt not commit adultery;

28. But I say unto you, that whosoever looketh on a woman, to lust after her, hath committed adultery already in his heart [thoughts].

29. Behold, I give unto you a commandment, that ye suffer none of these things to enter into

your heart [thoughts]... -- 3 Nephi 12:27-29, Matt 5:28

The next time such thoughts attempt to distract you, with something, such as: "Look at that sexy woman." Agree with the thought, ie: "Yes, she does have a sexy body." (Make sure the agreeing thought deals with the negative idea which has been presented to your mind.) "She is one of my beautiful sisters and I would defend her virtue with my life if I had to." Women can use the system in like manner.

As a woman, I have been surprised and shocked with thoughts which have attempted to attract my attention. I decided that I must always be on guard. I know of the mental battles. As the inner temptations have mentally approached me, I have learned to ask for light and knowledge to teach me. I have learned many useful safeguards and use them as tools or keys in my life. The Lord does answer prayers. Now, I share the key with all who have eyes to see, ears to hear and hearts that feel.

This is one of the many ways we can use to cut off the evil one. You have agreed that your sister does have a lovely shape, or that the men, our brothers, are handsome, but you did not dwell upon it. Instead, you have lifted the idea to a higher spiritual plane and have saved your own virtue within your own heart and thoughts. Alma teaches us that the Savior will judge us even for our thoughts. So it is time for us all to be more responsible by watching over every thought that tries to bring us down and influence our actions.

Situation #3

Every home and its family members will be under attack wherever they are weak. The evil one knows that the most powerful unit in the universe is a husband and wife who are of one mind and one heart and who work as one with the Lord. This great unit has the potential to go forth and become like unto God, and to create universes of their own, in the eternities. This being the greatest unit on earth, who would try to destroy every marriage possible? The Spoiler. He will try every marriage to the greatest degree, especially those sealed in the Holy Temples. And when trials come to your doorstep you might be tempted to think: "Oh, no. We must not be meant for each other."

Marriage is work! It is working together! It is the Gospel in action. Do you recall that when the Lord told us to forgive 70 times 7? He could have been referring to the home and family members. Only in the home do we allow anyone to repeat so many trespasses. We need to forgive many times, set boundaries, communicate and choose again until it is Love we Choose. We wouldn't let a friend or associate make 490 choices against us. Only in our homes do we come close to this number per topic. The greatest need to live the Gospel lies in the home.

A husband and wife might apply the Agree Technique in the following manner: The husband comes home from work, comes into the house, and notices that the living room isn't cleaned up from the kids playing. His first response might be:

"Why is the front room such a mess?" (Implied is: Can't

you keep the home tidy? You have been home all day!)

The husband or wife can choose to defend their self or to Agree. To defend yourself only turns into a hurtful argument, but to Agree with your spouse in some small way defuses the potential argument. One could reply in the following way:

"Yes, it is a mess! Would you help me clean up?

To speak of a workable compromise opens the door to validate the positive feelings that are wanted.

These techniques in the counseling world are called **Fogging, Broken Record,** and **Workable Compromise.** They really do work. The term "Fogging," is to: "Agree with thine adversary quickly," as discussed earlier. Our negatives can be turned into positives by these tools.

Satan addresses you in your mind as "You"

Since you now know that Satan speaks to you in your mind and that you most often hear him in your own tone of voice, you are ready to see that Satan addresses you as "you". When you speak to yourself about yourself, do you think of yourself as "you"'? Of course not! You think of yourself and address yourself as "I" and your self-talk is always by thought and spoken in that way. "I will do this" or "I like that."

This is one way you can know when the whisperings are from Satan. Learn to listen to your self-talk and discern whether you are hearing "you" or "I" spoken in your mind.

When you hear negative messages using the word "you", you can know these whisperings are from the Spoiler, the wicked one that is seeking to get you to listen to him so he can make you confused, double-minded, critical, or unhappy.

Another way you can know which spiritual web site you are going to is by how you feel about yourself and the world. Do your thoughts leave you feeling good and uplifted, or do they leave you feeling angry, depressed, and critical? If they are negative and destructive, you can know they are from the Spoiler.

Ask For Light And Knowledge

When you have problems, needs, or desires, the Lord would have you ask for Light and Knowledge, first to help you know if these are righteous desires D & C 46: 30- 33. And then He wants you to receive those things which are confirmed.

The story of the Brother of Jared is a good example. We learn in Ether 2:23-25 that when the Brother of Jared needed light for his boats he presented his problem to the Lord.

The Lord simply said: "What will ye that I should do that ye may have light in your vessels?" In verse 25 the Lord again asked: "Therefore what will ye that I should prepare for you that ye may have light when ye are swallowed up in the depths of the sea?"

In reality, the Lord is asking us to think about what we want Him to do for us. Then ask Him for that help. Too often we sit around and say, "Oh, thy will be done," when in fact the Lord is asking us to tell Him what we need so that He can help us. Working it out for yourself is a necessary part of this earth experience. We act as if the Lord requires us to hurt, when in fact hurt is an indication that there is an area where we need help from the Lord, to change it from a problem to a miracle.

The brother of Jared, in Ether 3:2 acknowledged his need to the Lord. He acknowledged in humble prayer that he knew that we must call upon the Lord in order that we may receive from him according to our desires.

> ...nevertheless, O Lord, thou hast given us a
> commandment that we must call upon thee, that
> from thee we may receive according to our desires.
> -- Ether 3:2

The Brother of Jared pointed out then in verse 4 that he knew that the Lord has all power and can do whatsoever he will for the benefit of man. He therefore petitioned the Lord to "...touch these stones, O Lord, with thy finger, and prepare them that they may shine forth in darkness; and they shall shine forth unto us in the vessels which we have prepared, that we may have lights while we shall cross the sea." (Ether 3:2)

His prayer was offered in total faith, for he knew that the Lord could do all things. He knew, therefore, that his request could be granted, since the request was for their good. And he received what he asked for because he asked in faith.

By following this example, we can start to have the righteous desires of our hearts granted to us.

Ask And Doubt Not

As we begin to understand what the Lord was saying in the previous passage in Ether, the scripture in Mark 11:23-24 begins to make more sense. In this scripture, the Lord isn't just talking about mountains or the sea, but about our problems, any and all of them and how we may transform them. He's telling us that when we ask in faith and doubt not that Christ lives then we shall receive whatsoever we ask.

23. For verily I say unto you, That whosoever shall say unto this mountain, [problem] Be thou removed, and be thou cast into the sea [be gone]; and shall not doubt in his heart [thoughts], but shall believe that those things which he saith shall come to pass; he shall have whatsoever he saith.

24. Therefore I say unto you, What things soever ye desire, when ye pray, believe that ye receive them, and ye shall have them. -- Mark 11:23-24

What a revelation! My soul is finally awakening, and I am beginning to recognize the real thought-power of my Positive Inner Self-Talk or my Faith, created by my Spirit Intelligence.

Assignments

Workbook pages are found on the following pages of this chapter. Please feel free to make copies of these work book pages for personal use.

*Workbook page instructions: Fill in the blanks then pray over these desires. Stay **single-minded** by using your Positive Inner Self-Talk. Think and speak only of these desires in the positive, present tense. **Erase all negative thoughts** which try to get your attention. Then ask until you receive your confirmed desire/goal. We call these results, a miracle.*

What are my hopes and desires?

Area #1 Husband – Wife

1._____ and I communicate well together.
2._____ is peaceful, happy and fun to be around.
3. Father, I desire to be of one mind and one heart with my husband or wife. I know that Christ lives and I Doubt HIM Not (Have the Spirit confirm this great desire. I feel that couples can grow closer by this request from the Father).

Area #2   Children or Extended Family Members

1. _____

Area #3 I Ask For Light and Knowledge:

1. Father, I Ask to understand how the Law of Faith Works?

2. Ask for anything you are pondering on or hurting over

_____

Area #4 Business – Job -- Earnings -- School -- Mission Money Needs -- Food Storage -- Get Out Of Debt

1. _____

2. _____

Area #5   Missionary work – Church Jobs – etc.

1. "Father in Heaven, we desire thy help to guide us to someone who will become interested in the Gospel message. We desire this to happen by _____."

(Is anything too hard for the Lord? It takes your Belief or Positive Inner Self-Talk and staying single minded.)

2. "Father, we ask thee to send forth Angels to put questions about thy Gospel into the minds of our friends. Wilt thou cause them to desire to ask us the questions then request to learn more. We desire that our friends might ask us if they could be taught by the missionaries and that they might pray and receive a witness from the Holy Ghost, then request to be baptized."

Sample Prayer Idea:

"Father, I seek help with my Righteous Desires (be specific). I ask for Light and Knowledge to come to me concerning them. I Doubt Not thy power and I know that all things are possible unto thee. (Ether 3:4) I thank Thee for all that Thou hast done for me in my life." Next ask specifically over a Hope. Zero in on something. Be patient. Keep asking as you erase each negative thought that would try to confuse and "Spoil" your ability to receive. You must keep single minded by your mental effort. Then the Lord opens the doors you cannot, and softens the Hearts of others, even of your sweetheart when needed. He creates the results which are miracles to us because we know that we could not have done them by ourselves. Then we feel JOY!

As I listened to the tapes, *Joseph Smith the Prophet*, by Truman Madsen, I noticed an interesting detail, where Joseph taught the Saints to: "Weary the Lord until He blesses you." In other words, "...men ought always to pray, and not to faint. " (St. Luke 18:1-8) Learn to "Ask" – "Seek" – "Knock" until He blesses you with the Righteous Desires of your Heart. This is the "Mommy, Mommy" principle you have noticed children use.

Your Faith Will Be Tried

The Joseph Smith translation of Hebrews 11:1 tells us that Faith is the *Assurance* of things hoped for, the *Proof* of things not seen. The above words help me apply a level of faith with full (assurance) that we may reap a harvest (proof at first not seen). After exerting your Faith, notice how negative thoughts try to get your attention. Positive thought is the *expression* of your Faith, but the opposite, or negative thought, is the *trial* of that exerted Faith.

Ether expresses this thought well. Says he:

Ye Receive No Witness Until After The Trial Of Your Faith – Ether 12:16

- Because faith is connected to Positive Thought, Negative thoughts will test you. i.e. "You are not good enough to ask and receive." The Spoiler's e-mail or evil mail arrives as a "You" message. So march forward to Delete the evil mail by "resisting the devil and he will flee from you" (James 4:7-8) then replace the negative with your positive confirmed desire.

- Keep Thinking Positive Thoughts In Your Mind About Your Hopes – (with assurance of Faith)
- Then Comes The Fruits Of Faith, Or Miracles. (This is the proof of Faith)

You can hope for things you do not see, and extend your Positive Mental Effort on it. Then when you ask, you will receive your righteous desires. It is time to start learning how to move our lives forward by Faith. Now is the time to have an Enoch experience, to start receiving what you ask for because of your Doubting Not Faith in Jesus Christ. He lives! We can start today to bind Satan in our own lives in preparation for this marvelous time on earth which the Prophets call the Millennium.

- Review the Outline of Lesson 2/Puzzle Piece #2 in Appendix I.

- Read the book "The Five Love Languages.: By Gary Chapman
- Research the courses within www.loveandlogic.com The Fay and Klien Institute

- "I Don't Have To Make Everything All Better." -- By Gary and Joy Lundberg.

PUZZLE PIECE #3
Ask – Seek – Knock

Ask Seek and Knock

Ask - Seek – Knock

How Can You Receive The Lord's Help To Achieve Your Hopes and Desires?

Joseph Smith Said to "Weary the Lord Until He Blesses You."

(Found in the Truman Madsen Tapes, *"Joseph Smith the Prophet"*)

Matthew 7:7-11 Let us learn more.

Ask, Seek, Knock

> 7. Ask, and it shall be given you; seek, and ye shall find; knock, and it shall be opened unto you:

> 8. For every one that asketh receiveth; and he that seeketh findeth; and to him that knocketh it shall be opened.

> 9. Or what man is there of you, whom if his son ask (for some) bread, will he give him a stone?

> 10. Or if he ask (for) a fish, will he give him a serpent?

> 11. If ye then, being evil, know how to give good gifts unto your children, how much more shall your father which is in heaven give good things to them that ask him? -- Matthew 7:7-11

A frequent instruction the Lord gives to us is that we should ask, and it shall be given to us, knock and it shall be opened unto us. And He points out that if we, being human, would give good gifts to our children, how much more shall the Father give good things to his children on earth, if they ask Him in prayer. The greater clarity came to me one day as I was substitute teaching in a high school computer class. The following thoughts entered like an email from the Lord = "Eternal Father Mail". On that special day, I heard...

"Ask" a question and the answers will be given to you.

"Seek," by asking a question and ye will find the answers.

"Knock," by asking a question and the doors of knowledge will be opened to you.

I wrote down this simple information that was clear and exciting to my heart. I had been pondering – Ask – Seek – Knock for many years and there it was so sweetly simplifide.

Ask a question – then follow up with what comes into your precious mind. Study, ponder, pray and ask for more Light and Knowledge as we walk through our Earth Life Schooling, following Jesus Christ.

"Ask The Lord
And He Will Instruct You"

General Conference is always such a rich outpouring of the Spirit that many times truths of real value go almost unnoticed.

Here is an incident recounted by Brother Theodore M. Burton of the First Quorum of the Seventy, which was published in the Ensign for November 1985, p. 64. He told of an experience which happened to him which helped him to understand better how the Lord speaks into our mind and heart.

I was called to be a General Authority twenty-five years ago and had no idea at first what I would be asked to do. I was assigned to hold a stake conference the very next weekend and went for advice to my former stake president, Elder Harold B. Lee, who was then a member of the Council of the Twelve Apostles. I asked him to tell me what to do. His answer both shocked and frightened me. He said, "Theodore, you are a General Authority now. No one tells a General Authority how to act in his special calling. If you have questions, ask the Lord and He will instruct you." I had prayed before, never expecting a direct answer, but now I prayed soberly and with real intent.

The Lord did answer my prayers—not in ways I expected, but by speaking things into my mind. But that only happened after I had studied the problem and prepared myself to receive an answer. I have been startled by some of the things that have come to me. Scriptures I had not understood before suddenly were made meaningful. Answers I had previously passed over in reading the scriptures took on new significance. I have truly learned over these years line upon line and precept upon precept. I have learned to follow living prophets as well as those prophets who have passed on. Of necessity I have learned to live by faith.

D&C 8:2-4 explains that the Lord speaks into your mind by the Holy Ghost. This truth becomes very powerful in our lives as each of us attune ourselves to the spirit of the Lord by listening. Our job is to become clean and PURE in our HEART (thoughts) so that we, "by your Faith" can begin to inherit the blessings and visions and glories of God. In Ether 4:13-16 we learn that there is knowledge which is hid up because of our unbelief. (Unbelief has stopped us?) By shifting our mental gears to a BELIEF thought pattern we can turn our lives around and begin to receive inspiration, light and knowledge from the Lord.

Isn't this what Nephi did? Yes! Nephi asked for help when he did not understand the dreams of his prophet father, Lehi. Laman and Lemuel simply doubted then allowed their unbelief to rob them of the Light and Knowledge from the Lord. If they had truly desired to know, they could have asked in faith: "Father, we do not understand. We ask for Light and Knowledge. Wilt thou teach us?" Then the Lord would have taught them also. To question is not wrong, but to question then not ask for an answer is unbelief.

Nephi Teaches Us

> 20. ... I, Nephi, will show unto you that the tender mercies of the Lord are over all those whom he hath chosen, because of their faith, to make them mighty even unto the power of deliverance. -- Nephi 1:20

The Lord chooses us by the Faith we show. He doesn't create favorites.

We Must Weary The Lord: The Parable of the Unjust Judge

> 1. And he spake a parable unto them to this end, that men ought always to pray, and not to faint;

> 2. Saying, there was in a city a judge, which feared not God, neither regarded man:

> 3. And there was a widow in that city; and she came unto him, saying, Avenge me of mine adversary.

> 4. And he would not for a while: but afterward he said within himself, though I fear not God, nor regard man;

5. Yet because this widow troubleth me, I will avenge her, lest by her continual coming she weary me.

6. And the Lord said, Hear what the unjust judge saith.

7. And shall not God avenge his own elect, which cry day and night unto him, though he bear long with them?

8. I tell you that he will avenge them speedily. Nevertheless when the Son of man cometh, shall he find faith on the earth? -- St. Luke 18:1-8

It appears that if we have "Faith", it will show by being persistent in presenting our confirmed righteous desires unto the Lord in prayer, until we receive them. On page 105 of this material, you will find a quote from *The Lost Books of the Bible*. This passage points out that if you do not receive what you ask for from the Lord it is because you stopped asking or you allowed doubting thoughts to enter your mind. Thus, you become double-minded to the extent that you can receive nothing from the Lord (James 1:5-8). It also points out the fact that doubting thoughts are received from the devil or spoiler.

Rend The Veil Of Unbelief – Then Shall My Revelations Be Unfolded

Let us examine the passage in Ether more carefully.

15. Behold, when ye shall rend that veil of unbelief

which doth cause you to remain in your awful state of wickedness, and hardness of heart, and blindness of mind, then shall the great and marvelous things which have been hid up from the foundation of the world from you—yea, when ye shall call upon the Father in my name, with a broken heart [thoughts turned to the Lord] and a contrite spirit [being teachable], then shall ye know that the Father hath remembered the covenant which he made unto your fathers, O house of Israel.

16. And then shall my revelations which I have caused to be written by my servant John be unfolded in the eyes of all the people. --Ether 4:15-16

We, by our faith, are the generation which can make this happen. My soul hurts as I observe the wickedness of our times. The Spoiler is working overtime but we by our unbelief are giving him power. It is time to switch our "mental gears", and to increase our Faith in the Lord Jesus Christ, through whom all things are possible, even to the extent of overcoming the wickedness of our time. We are told in 1 John 5:4 that we will overcome the world (or the wicked) by our FAITH. (The term "world" is defined as "wicked" in Joseph Smith –Matthew vs. 4.)

4. For whatsoever is born of God [have a broken heart and a contrite spirit] overcometh the world [the wicked]: and this is the victory that overcometh the world, even our faith.

5. Who is he that overcometh the world, but he that believeth that Jesus is the Son of God? --1 John 5:4-5

Why Repentance Is Needed

The Lord has told the Prophets to teach nothing but repentance unto this people. Why? Is it because by doing so we start the process of becoming **Pure in Heart** (in **thought**)? As we purify our thoughts (**The Real Part of us or our Intelligence**), we also purify our emotions and actions, which puts us into the situation of being able to ask the Lord for Spirit Confirmed desires and to receive them. Enoch, together with his whole city, learned to be of **One Mind and One heart** and they received all that they asked for. I wonder if they decided as a group what their **Righteous Desires** would be, then individually and unitedly presented their desires to the Lord. ALL were willing to be united, to pray daily for the same things and they received them because of their unwavering, undoubting single-minded **Faith in Jesus Christ**.

6. And, as it is written – Whatsoever ye shall ask in faith, being united in prayer according to my command, ye shall receive. -- D&C 29:6

It is time for our generation to also learn to bind Satan, as did the people of the city of Enoch. We must learn to listen to him no more in our hearts. We *can* unite and be of one heart and one mind (thought), by using our mental efforts through our prayers, as we go forth and decide to live the gospel truths. We can unite in our sincere desire to halt the evil which covers the land. We can ask the Lord to put it into the minds of our leaders to halt the pornography which fills the internet the movies, videos, magazines, music and TV.

Then we can individually do whatever we feel impressed is correct. *We must* stand up and be counted.

The Deutsche Democratic Republic (East Germany) Opened Up Through The Faith Of All The Members' Prayers

Members throughout the Church have been asked to pray that the hearts of the leaders be softened in the nations which had not yet allowed our missionaries in. We asked in faith (for we know that Jesus Christ lives and we *doubt Him not*). Faithful members unitedly asked in faith that the way might be opened up, and this prayer of faith was heard. Pres. Thomas S. Monson, Second Counselor to President Benson, reported in General Conference, April 1989 (Ensign, May 1989, p. 50-53) that Church leaders had met with the leaders of that land and the way was opened up at that time for chapels to be built, a temple of God to be constructed, and for members of the church in that country to be allowed to have missionaries come and start teaching the people, and for missionaries there to be allowed out of their land to serve where called.

Chairman Honecker, representing the German leadership said, "We know you. We trust you. We have had experience with you. Your missionary request is approved." The leaders' hearts had been softened. And yes, the faith and devotion of the members in that nation had not gone unnoticed by our loving Father and God of all.

Listen again to what the Lord says in D&C 29:6: "And as it is written – Whatsoever ye shall ask in faith (I know Christ Lives and I Doubt Him Not), being united in prayer according to my command, ye shall receive."

In Ether 3:2 we read, "Nevertheless, O Lord, Thou has

given us a commandment that we must call upon thee, that from thee we may receive according to our desires." May Ether's words awaken a desire in you to learn the laws of faith. Where do you begin to use them in the right ways?

The Ten Steps of Faith

1. Recognize a desire or a challenge.
2. Think and ponder about how you desire to solve the challenge. In prayer ask for light and knowledge in regards to its accomplishment. Now ideas can come from the Spirit into your mind. Listen and immediately do whatever the Spirit directs you to do.
3. Choose a desire and then ask: Is this desire for my good?" You may feel a positive emotional impression, a feeling of "yes " within you, or even better, the burning or tingling of the Spirit. You may feel a negative impression or a stupor of thought which indicates a "no." Correct the request until you receive a "yes" confirmation. (See: D & C 46:7-9, 23, 30.)
4. Wait for the answer. Answers come in many ways:
   - A burning in the soul. D & C 9:8
   - Instructions received as thoughts in the mind. (D & C 8:2-4; Enos 1:10)
   - Feelings of peace. (D & C 6:22 -23.)
   - Instructions in dreams.
   - Positive ideas which stay in the mind. (D & C 128:1.)
5. As the Spirit confirms your desire, it becomes God's will for you, "wherefore it is done even as he asketh." (D & C 46:30.) Now, write it down.
6. Use the following procedure to spiritually release the confirmed desire into the Lord's hands.

Ask:

- "Would I release this confirmed desire to the Lord, if I felt I could?" (Answer "yes.")
- "Could I release it through my faith in Jesus Christ to help me?" (Answer "yes.")
- "When will I let it go into the Lord's hands and release it to be fulfilled in the Lord's own time for me?" (Answer "now.")
- Give Thanks – with your inner-self talk saying, I Thank Thee – I Thank Thee – I Thank Thee.

Now do the following:

- In your prayers just say, "I thank thee for the (speak what you are asking for) which is coming. (In this statement, you are saying that you are hoping for something you do not see which the Spirit has confirmed.)
- Doubt not in your heart or thoughts.
- Be aware that your faith will be tried at this time through negative thoughts or situations.
- Say, "I choose to release these negative thoughts," or use the "Would I?" "Could I?" "When?" procedure as shown above.
- Now, listen to the positive ideas or impressions from the Spirit as it guides you and do what it confirms.
7. Persist in prayer and follow the impressions of the Spirit until you receive your confirmed desire.
8. According to the Lord's timetable, you shall receive your desire through your faith in Jesus Christ.
9. Feel the joy of having your righteous desires come to

pass or reflect on what you can learn when they do not come to pass when you wanted.

10. Give thanks in all things and start again.

By this procedure, I do not mean to imply that you should submit your order to the Lord, and then put your life on hold, focusing all your energy into the request until He delivers it. Instead, determine a righteous desire, then persist peacefully in faith and prayer as you continue with your life. It is also a misunderstanding to assume that you choose one desire and avoid approaching the Lord with any other until that one is fulfilled. It may be that the goal or righteous desire you have chosen to focus on will not be fulfilled until the Millennium! The idea is to consistently determine many righteous desires to present to the Lord in faith, and then trust in the Lord's timetable for their fulfillment.

This is only one clear pattern through which the Lord can work with us. You may follow the example of others who have used these and many other oaths of faith and were blessed with joy for doing so.

Missionaries in North Germany Ask, Seek, and Knock

Sister Carrie Roquemore of Brighton, Colorado, and Kimberly Batchelor of Mesa, Arizona served together for a number of months. Both were eager to learn, grow, to build their understanding of the gospel so that they might have a rich and rewarding mission. They decided that they could do so by concentrating on faith, the first principle of the gospel. I quote from their letter to me:

As Sister Batchelor and I began our intense study of faith, we began to listen to your tape, "Faith

Unpuzzled," every day. We also began to find a lot of information in the scriptures and in the other books (A Marvelous Work and A Wonder by LeGrand Richards by James E. Talmage and the Articles of Faith). Whenever we'd find something of interest or significance during our personal study, we'd share it and discuss it. As our understanding deepened, we noticed something happening to us. Faith was no longer something mysterious that just happened. We began to see that the level of our faith climbed higher and with increased faith we were able to do more with that. We were in control! What a heady sensation that was! We could do something about it!

As we applied the simple steps and exercises we learned from our study, and as we took upon ourselves direct responsibility for our thoughts, and consequently our actions, the miracles started occurring. The principles we followed were:

1. We watched over our thoughts and practiced mentally replacing all negative thoughts with positive thoughts.
2. We wrote out your desires and asked if they were the Lord's will.
3. When the Spirit revealed that they are for our good, we persisted in prayer until we received our desire.
4. We mentally casteth out all doubting thoughts in order to focus on our most persistent thought. As we did this, we were doing our part; now the Lord could do his part, for we

were being single-minded!

Some people say that North Germans are a cold people. I can understand why there is this misconception. When we did street contacting, most often the people would simply walk by without acknowledging our existence. Many times they were rude and brusque. But as we began applying ourselves to the task of controlling our thoughts, keeping them positive, seeing only the good, and pushing away and eventually clearing the negative influences, a wonderful thing happened. Not only did our love for these people grow deeper and purer, that same love entered our companionship. We made our own discovery, that this positive mind-set leads to a well of pure Christlike love. And, of course, everyone around us could feel it, too.

As we applied our positive faith to our proselyting skills, the people responded beautifully. Before we knew it, we had over thirty new people in our teaching pool simply because of our increased faith and knowledge that this was the Lord's work and that he would bless us with success.

One day, during an incredible cold snap, we bundled up to do our regular morning street contacting followed by tracting in apartment buildings. From previous experience, we knew mornings were not a good time to tract, and we were loathe to give up on our street contacting. Even though there was the possibility of frozen limbs, we decided to talk to just a few more people.

The Lord blessed us because of our determination. The next person we talked to was a mother with two children in tow. She stopped readily and immediately invited us over to talk to her husband the next Saturday. She was a beautiful woman who had been looking into every religion searching for the truth. She suffered traumatic blows in her personal life not long after hearing our message and could have become disillusioned or disheartened, but she kept the faith and accepted the baptismal challenge.

As we became more confident in our understanding of faith and our ability to call upon the Lord, we decided to take up a challenge by President Taylor. He told us we should not only pray to be led to those chosen and ready brothers and sisters, but that we should pray to have them led to us! When I first heard that statement, I remember thinking, "yeah, right!" But now it didn't seem at all unrealistic. We took Elder Taylor's challenge to heart and within the first few days two young women came up to us and asked us if we could come and tell them more about the Church. The principle of faith at work is really powerful.

Sincerely,

Sister Roquemore and Sister Batchelor

Mormon Teaches Us About Miracles

Mormon teaches us that Miracles are real and only our unbelief (doubting thoughts) stops us.

18. And who shall say that Jesus Christ did not do

many mighty miracles? And there were many mighty miracles wrought by the hands of the apostles.

19. And if there were miracles wrought then, why has God ceased to be a God of miracles and yet be an unchangeable Being? And behold, I say unto you he changeth not; if so he would cease to be God; and He ceaseth not to be God, and is a God of miracles.

20. And the reason why he ceaseth to do miracles among the children of men is because that they <u>dwindle in unbelief</u>, and <u>depart from the right way, and know not the God in whom they should trust.</u>

There Is a RIGHT WAY to ASK for our Desires

21. Behold, I say unto you that whoso believeth in Christ, doubting nothing, whatsoever he shall ask the Father in the name of Christ it shall be granted him; and this promise is unto all, even unto the ends of the earth. -- Mormon 9:18-21, also read vs. 25, 27-28.

Each of us must fine-tune our Doubting Not Faith in Jesus Christ, to be able to cause the Laws of Faith to work for our good. We must ask in the Right Way!

We Are The Generation Who Can Learn How To Bind The Spoiler!

I desire with all my soul to see our generation learn to do this, to bind the Spoiler in our minds and to stop the filth that is shouted from the housetops into our homes via Cable TV, Satellite and Internet.

3. And the rebellious shall be pierced with much sorrow; for *their iniquities shall be spoken upon the housetops,* and their secret acts shall be revealed.

-- D&C 1:3

The children of our present generation have been told that because of their strength they have been saved to come forth now at this time upon the earth, just before the Second Coming of Christ. I would also include their parents among these valiant souls, for we, the parents, must be prepared to teach our "Saturday Warriors" so that they can perform their callings in these Last Days.

However, I am concerned regarding this call to be valiant, as I see and hear of the battles daily fought in the schools. Instead of being valiant some of our latter-day army are giving into the forces of evil.

"What?" you might ask! "How can that be?" Consider this: If about 50% of our LDS teenagers and elementary school children are using vulgar language, right along with the kids of the world (world=wicked), and are going to the nude PG, PG13, R rated movies, and watching other vulgar media, often with Latter-day Saint parents or advisors as chaperones, then are we fulfilling our commitment? Can we feel ourselves to be the Latter-Day army of the Lord? No!

Why do some Priesthood fathers allow their teenage sons to have Playboy Magazines? And then their only reprimand is that "Boys will be boys." Do we recognize that this is only the beginning of our sorrow? For always, as you sow, "so shall ye reap." We have missionaries in the field who have a real struggle with vulgar language because they had not learned to control their thoughts and their tongue before they left home. Now how can the Lord work through an unclean vessel? It is hard! We must clean up our lives.

Remember that the "Spoiler" works by whispering into your ears Negative, Doubting, Evil, or Fearful Thoughts. If you are hearing filthy words in your mind then you are tuned into the wrong internet server and website operated by the evil one. We cannot have filthy thoughts and be in tune with the Holy Ghost. We are living here in physical bodies but fighting a spiritual battle within your Mind, Heart and Thoughts. We are not just a body, but we are Thought-Intelligence (Spirit Beings), inside our mortal body. We must always watch over our thoughts so that we can become the person we Desire to become. We are told in 1 John 3:2-3 that if we have the Hope of seeing the Savior when He comes, then we must purify ourselves, even as the Savior is pure.

Our earth life is a very humbling experience. Almost daily I have to deal with Negative or Evil Thoughts in my mind. It is not our near-perfectness, but rather our effort to have constant watch over our thoughts which makes us able to come to the Lord and ask for the Desires of our Hearts. We take the Sacrament each week to cleanse us of our sins of the past week and to help us get through the next week of our lives. I have heard many people respond, "But I do not feel as though I am worthy to receive my desires." Here is a scripture which could put you at rest.

> 7. But ye are commanded in all things to ask of God, who giveth liberally; and that which the Spirit testifies unto you even so I would that ye should do in all holiness of heart, walking uprightly before me,

considering the end of your salvation, doing all things with prayer and thanksgiving, that ye may not be seduced by evil spirits, or doctrines of devils, or the commandments of men; for some are of men, and others of devils.

8. Wherefore, beware lest ye are deceived; and that ye may not be deceived seek ye earnestly the best gifts, always remembering for what they are given;

9. For verily I say unto you, they are given for the benefit of those who love me and keep all my commandments, and him that seeketh so to do; that all may be benefited that seek or that ask of me, that ask and not for a sign that they may consume it upon their lusts. -- D&C 46:7-9

We do fit in. As we are seeking to live the commandments the Lord will listen and answer our prayers.

We Can Ask For Gifts Of The Spirit

Each of us can ask for spiritual Gifts by our prayer of faith. Please turn to D & C Section 46 and examine verse 23. One of the spiritual gifts we have been discussing is mentioned here. "And to others the discerning of spirits." To fine-tune your reception of the Spirit is a gift, one which is needed by every person upon the earth so that we are not deceived.

Verse 30 is a marvelous and powerful scripture for us to realize. It teaches that: "He that asketh in the spirit asketh according to the will of God; wherefore it is done even as he asketh." I take my righteous desires to the Lord at home and to the Temple at times to get a confirmation by the Spirit. I have received a witness in different ways. At times I have had a burning in the soul or a tingling feeling (D&C 9:8) and other times a Peace confirms my request, or I hear the inner still small voice which actually speaks within me. The common result is that when the Spirit confirms my request, then I know that the desire is now God's will and it is done even as I have asked. I then weary the Lord until the miracle occurs, plus I say daily, "I thank Thee for this marvelous system of faith and for the blessings which are confirmed and coming." I know, without a doubt that our confirmed desires are on the way, I just do not know how and allow them to reveal themselves.

Moroni describes this system whereby we may lay hold upon every good thing. Says he:

> 25. Wherefore, by the ministering of angels, and by every word which proceeded forth out of the mouth of God, men began to exercise faith in Christ; and thus by faith, *they did lay hold upon every good thing;* and thus it was until the coming of Christ.

> 26. And after that he came men also were saved by faith in his name; and by faith, they become the sons of God. And as surely as Christ liveth he spake these words unto our fathers, saying: Whatsoever thing ye shall ask the Father in my name, which is good, in faith believing that ye shall receive, behold, it shall be done unto you. -- Moroni 7:25-26

Always Remember That Your Thoughts Direct

Your Life

Remember that thought is one way to create emotion, and emotion creates the action of your physical body. As you watch over your thoughts you will be given the emotions you self directed. As you repeat over and over in your mind that you forgive someone of his trespasses against you or your family, you will start to feel the emotion of forgiveness. It will grow and become a controlling force in your life. You can then take the next step of your Desire, and self-feed into your mind the thought-pattern that "I love (you), I love (you), I love (you)", and keep repeating this over and over. As you do, you will discover that you will start to feel love again for that individual. Loving others goes well with setting boundaries – communicating better and becoming wiser in relationships. Then realize that you have placed *yourself* in control instead of allowing the Spoiler to be in charge of your life. You can control your life through this type of creative thinking, that is, by using your Mental Effort. Here are four of my favorite steps. First think of the person or situation in mind, then sincerely say:

- I am sorry.
- Please forgive me.
- I love you.
- Thank you.

We are not alone. We just need to start tuning into the Lord's Internet-Server. *We Can Do It! We Must Learn to Do It!* We are the trusted ones. We told Him before we came to earth that we *would* do it. Let us go forth then, with faith and determination, true to that Self within, our Thought Intelligence/Spirit. *Now is the time. Let us begin!*

Repentance And Forgiveness – Cleansing The Inner Vessel

Repentance and forgiveness are important principles in the learning of faith and joy. Ask, Seek, Knock – and learn also how to repent and to forgive.

As I repent of my ill fated choices, I will choose again until it is Love I choose, I will take the steps necessary for repentance. First comes recognition and sorrow, then confession (to the Lord and to the person whom I have wronged plus the Bishop when needed), and offering that person whatever restitution that I can. Finally, I can then be prepared to forgive myself of that choice. And as I do I will be able to Transform my subconscious mind, and simply use it as a learning experience, to help me avoid making that choice again.

Here is an important principle of learning. As problems arrive, become awake, learn to make choices that can bring to you the results you want. The Lord has said that you can ask for His forgiveness and help in solving them. With wisdom and spiritual gifts in place – that choice can be corrected for a more pure choice.

But there is also another most important step in order to be totally freed of that choice and that guilt. You must learn to forgive yourself. Until you can forgive yourself, you will not be able to love yourself. If you are not able to forgive and love yourself, how then will you ever be able to love another? The Lord has taught us that "Thou shalt love thy neighbor as thyself." This is literally true. You can only love your neighbor as you learn to love yourself.

We are often harder on ourself than we are on another.

The Spoiler and you keep bringing up the unfruitful choices that you have made, rehashing and reliving them. This is what guilt is made of – the lack of repentance and forgiveness on your own part allows the evil one to can mentally trigger your memory again and again.

You will never be able to be cleansed within until you have learned to repent and to forgive, both yourself and others. That is why this next exercise and assignment on the following page is so important. In it we share ways to "Erase and Replace", to erase the choice called sin or the ill thought of which you have been guilty, and since nature abhors a vacuum, to replace it immediately with something of a positive, pure, and enlightening nature.

You may read this "Erase and Replace" script to yourself each night just before you go to bed. You may make a recording of it or purchase the CD. This material is also available for purchase and can be downloaded to your iPad, or MP3 player, by going to my website: www.faithunpuzzled.com. Just read or listen to the "I Erase & Replace" as you retire. Play it faithfully each night for the next 21 nights. Then when you feel a need to repeat it, due to negative situations, you can return to it to release the negative thoughts and replace them with positive thoughts.

Do not be too disturbed if you find yourself dropping off to sleep in the middle of your recording. Your faithful subconscious mind is still hearing, recording, and storing this self-talk. Your subconscious mind is busy cleansing the inner vessel, clearing away the guilt and fear which you have harbored for so long. You will find, as you continue to use it, that you are feeling more cheerful, less subject to depression, moodiness, and fears. You are actually fortifying yourself against the onslaught of the Spoiler. You are putting YOU in charge, rather than allowing him to be in control. What a good and strengthening experience this can be! *You are becoming in charge of you* through listening to the positive, pure and enlightening Still Small Voice of the Spirit.

I Erase And Replace

Instructions:

1. Read this positive affirmation aloud each night for 21 nights in a row if possible.

2. After 21 days, the program is reaffirmed by you saying, "I Erase. . .and Replace." Say it as you retire each night or when you are in a situation you desire to Clear. Read very slowly, or listen to it as you retire. Begin by speaking out loud...

I feel relaxed . . . so relaxed . . . as I slowly drift into a most satisfying state of relaxation . . . All mental or physical tension is now Cleared . . . I Erase it . . . As it dissipates . . . I feel the warmth of my body . . . as my blood flows freely . . . circulating and bringing health . . . Daily relaxation is good for me . . . As I rest . . . I now direct the Erasing from my storage banks . . . every unhappy experience of my past along with the feelings of sorrow connected to them . . . even all negative reactions connected to them . . . I happily and easily let them go . . . I Release and Clear Myself . . . I am becoming a Positive part of this time upon the Earth . . . I am grateful for every experience I have had.

I know that each experience is a stepping stone to greater

knowledge and can be turned for my good . . . I now forgive myself for every negative choice I have ever made . . . I realize that when I am guilty of making a negative choice . . . I follow the Lord's Law of repentance . . . that of recognition . . . sorrow . . . confession . . . restitution when I can . . . asking for forgiveness . . . Then I am guilty only of learning . . . I know that out of each experience in life . . . good must surely come to me . . . I grow stronger with each experience . . . I am strong . . . with the Lord by my side. . . We are stronger than anything life can offer . . . The full application of the principle of repentance and forgiveness . . . now allows me to forgive myself for every negative choice I have ever made . . . I forgive myself . . . I forgive anyone who has ever wronged me or hurt me in any way . . . This Gospel principle of forgiveness . . . releases me from any negative feelings of self-dislike . . . I love myself... I love my neighbor as myself... The joy of myself- acceptance . . . is now felt in my powerful subconscious and gives me that power needed to love others . . . I accept myself . . . I accept others as they are . . . my self-acceptance frees me to be able to change that which must be changed . . . to grow and improve . . . in areas I desire . . . I am an amazing brilliant soul.

I let go of any fears which unjustly rule my life . . . I LOVE LIFE. . . this is a Happy day. . . People are a Joy to me . . . I need them . . . and they need me . . . I am a valuable, talented human being . . . I am aware of my great worth; . . . there are things to be done by me . . . which are done better by me than by any other person . . . There is no one who can exactly duplicate me . . . I AM PLEASED . . . I LOVE MYSELF . . . I ACCEPT MYSELF . . . I accept myself completely . . . I am free . . . free to be me completely, within the Gospel plan.

Now, because I have supplied myself with these priceless qualities and feelings . . . of love, forgiveness and acceptance . . I now have them to give . . . I give them freely . . . I now feel a sweet joyful sense of self love and self-determination filling my life . . . every waking and sleeping hour. . . . MY LIFE IS A JOY TO ME!

I now enjoy restful sleep and arise when I must . . . renewed and refreshed . . . I now Release and Clear Myself. I ERASE . . . AND REPLACE.

Paul said: ... "but be ye transformed by the renewing of your mind,..." --Romans 12:2

"The Lord Is My Light," . . . not the problems of the world. What I THINK ABOUT is what I TREASURE on earth. So I Think about my Hopes, and Desires to bring them about by My FAITH in Jesus Christ.

Assignment

1) Read the book – "Visions of Glory." By John Pontius - Publication Date: **November 13, 2012**

PUZZLE PIECE #4
Doubting Nothing

Carolyn P. Ringger

Doubting Nothing

Nothing Wavering!
No Doubting Thoughts!
Your Faith Will Be Tried!

Do I receive what I am asking for?

What is being Double Minded?

Being Double Minded

You are "Double Minded" if you listen to both spiritual radio-like stations or Internet servers. You actually shut the door on the Light, the "Inspiration" from the Lord as you pick up the "Sinspiration" or Negative Thoughts which can only attract what you do not want in your life.

All Discoveries Show Us What Nature Already Has In Place
I Have Noticed Two Internet-like Servers
Operating In Our Universe!

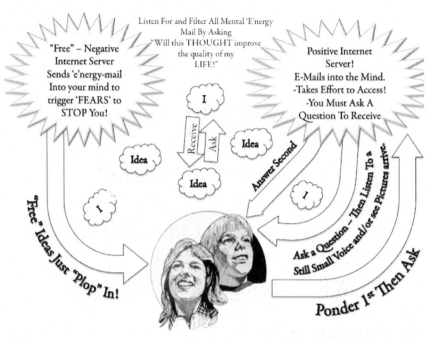

Listen For and Filter All Mental 'E'nergy Mail By Asking "Will this THOUGHT improve the quality of my LIFE!"

"Free" – Negative Internet Server Sends 'e'nergy-mail Into your mind to trigger 'FEARS' to STOP You!

Positive Internet Server! E-Mails into the Mind. -Takes Effort to Access! -You Must Ask A Question To Receive

I

Idea

Receive

Ask

Idea

Idea

Answer Second

I

"Free" Ideas Just "Plop" In!

Ask a Question – Then Listen To a Still Small Voice and/or see Pictures arrive.

Ponder 1st Then Ask

To Let Go Of A Thought Just Say: "I Delete That Thought!"

I Can DELETE
- Cuss words that arrive
- Ideas to lie, cheat or steal
- Immoral thoughts + desire
To look at pornography!

Ask a question and it shall be given you.

Seek by asking a question and ye shall find.

Knock by asking a question and it shall be opened to you.

Life IS Like A Game Of Hide and Go Seek!
All Truth Hides Waiting for us to Discover It!

Matthew 6:24 expresses the experience like this.

> 24. No man can serve two masters: for either he will hate the one, and love the other; or else he will hold to the one, and despise the other. Ye cannot serve God and mammon. -- Matthew 6:24

You are double minded when you:

1. Feel unjustified fear in your life.
2. Feel depressed due to allowing negative thoughts to flow in your mind.
3. Do not get along with your spouse.
4. Are offended too easily.
5. Have no communication between family members or missionary companions.
6. Have feelings of self-dislike.
7. Lose the desire to grow or to do missionary work if you are a missionary.
8. Stop caring about others.
9. Do not have your personal prayers morning and night. If you do not daily attune yourself to inspiration from the Lord, the spoiler's Internet Server will be blaring unrequested. The negative thought-giver does not believe in **Agency**. He forces himself upon your mind, then tells you that you created the filthy thoughts, and tries to have you feel that you are no good, when he is the one doing it all. He wants you and me to fail our earth test. Unless we rule over our thoughts, we are like a city without protection. (See Proverbs 25:28)
10. You are actually double-minded if you do not receive

the righteous desires of your heart which have been confirmed by the Spirit. Joseph Smith explained:

Because faith is wanting, the fruits are. No man since the world was had faith without having something along with it. The ancients quenched the violence of fire, escaped the edge of the sword, women received their dead, etc. By faith the worlds were made. A man who has none of the gifts has no faith; and he deceives himself, if he supposes he has. --Teachings Of The Prophet Joseph Smith, p. 270

11. Be not deceived; God is not mocked: for whatsoever a man soweth, that shall he also reap. -- Galatians 6:7

Thoughts are the seeds you sow.
You are the farmer and the harvester!

You Are A Mental Gardener
You plant seeds of thought daily in your life.

If in your backyard garden ...
- -- You plant PEAS, what will you get?
- -- If you plant CORN, what will you get?
- -- If you plant BEANS, what will you get?

Also according to the law of the harvest, you will reap only what you sow. As you plant one kernel of corn, will you get only one kernel back? No. You receive an abundance back.
So it is with you thoughts.

As A Mental Gardener in life,

if you plant (or think) thoughts such as:

1. I have no friends.
2. I am dumb.
3. I am fat.
4. I am Ugly.
5. I have an unhappy marriage.
6. I am not a good parent.
7. I hate Life!

Or if a missionary thinks ...

1. I can't teach as well as my companion.
2. I can't memorize the lessons or scriptures.
3. No one wants to listen to us.
4. We can't find people to teach.
5. I do not feel spiritual.
6. I can't stand my companion.
7. I do not like house-to-house contacting.
8. I hate my mission!

What Will You Get Back

You and I have literally planted seeds of thought which can only give us back an increase of its own kind, even an abundance. And if it be negative, then we will find our harvest to be in the reverse of what we think we want. "As a man thinketh in his heart, so is he." How very true that is. Negative thoughts attract negative experiences and positive thoughts attract positive experiences. Which do you want?

Negative thoughts will only trigger Faith into... A backward Motion.

Like Attracts Like

Your thoughts actually constitute electrical energy. You attract what you continually think about, as James 3:12 points out. He asks, can we get figs from an olive tree? Those thoughts which come to you are the kind which you have been thinking. "We are like human magnets," Elder Sterling W. Sill points out. "Our deeds, our attitudes, and even our thoughts attract in kind. Like begets like." (From *The Laws Of Success*, Ch. 7, by Sterling W. Sill)

In *The Neuropsychology of Achievement*, Steven DeVore, discusses the workings of the brain in relation to learning and achievement. DeVore discusses the above concepts. Though we do not see each other's thoughts, he explains, they exist in reality. They are composed of electromagnetic wave forms which possess energy and matter.

Thought is matter! Wow! According to the laws of quantum physics your visual images, created by your thoughts, are matter. Whatever clear image you visualize of yourself in your thoughts, is translated by your nervous system to be real, for thought is real. Thus if you will daily imagine yourself as a successful, healthy, lean and trim, happy person, and pre-live that way of life in your thoughts or mind's eye, those thoughts become the blueprint for your brain and body's nervous system. Your Self tells your Servo-mechanism how you desire it to serve You.

Negative thoughts likewise attract in the same way. The brain does not care what thoughts it receives, only that it serves you by attracting to you your most persistent thoughts. The brain is a servant, a gift from God and you are the instructor, and through your thoughts, you are the programmer. Therefore, you have a very important responsibility to watch over your thoughts.

King Benjamin teaches us regarding this in Mosiah 4:30. He instructs us to . . . "Watch over your thoughts, your words and your deeds...even unto the end of your lives,...that ye perish not."

How To Mentally Stay Single-Minded?

- D&C 4:5 Reminds Us That You Need To: "Keep Your Eye (Thoughts) Single To The Glory Of God"
- To Know That "Jesus Christ Lives And Doubt Him Not" Can Help To Fulfill This Desire!
- Watch Out For Double-Mindedness As If It Were A Disease.
- It Can Stop Inspiration And Miracles From Coming To You.

The Lord in D&C 67:1-3 warns us concerning our fears. (Fear is another form of double-mindedness.) Says he:

1. Behold and hearken, O ye elders of my church, who

have assembled yourselves together, whose prayers I have heard, and whose hearts I know, and whose desires have come up before me.

2. Behold and lo, mine eyes are upon you, and the heavens and the earth are in mine hands, and the riches of eternity are mine to give.

3. Ye endeavored to believe that ye should receive the blessing which was offered unto you; but behold, verily I say unto you there were fears in your hearts, *and verily this is the reason that ye did not receive.*
-- D&C 67:1-3

Fear is an insidious form of double-mindedness. The forces of evil only need to whisper something into your ear (mind) to trigger the emotion of fear. This will cause doubting and double-mindedness in your heart and mind unless you use your faith to act immediately. If you allow the fear to stay, however, then you can receive nothing from the Lord.

The prophet Job was sorely tested in this respect. He said: "For the thing which I greatly feared is come upon me, and that which I was afraid of is come unto me." --Job 3:25

Could it be that these things came upon him because of his doubting and fear?

To Receive You Must Doubt Not
If You Think Wavering or Negative Thoughts about Your Hopes-Desires,

You can receive nothing From the Lord. James says:
6. But let him ask in faith, nothing wavering. For he that wavereth is like a wave of the sea driven with the wind and tossed.

7. For let not that man think that he shall receive any thing of the Lord. --James 1:6-7

Doubting Nothing

Realize that to hope for something you cannot see is like the parable of the mustard seed. That seed may be so small it can hardly be seen. But all you have to do is plant the seed, nurture it and *it will grow.* The same is true of your Hopes and Desires, as you speak them to the Lord and mentally Doubt Not, they too will take root and grow. For you have planted and nourished a righteous desire through your (unseen) thoughts and faith.

In the terminology of modern science, you have set up an automatic electromagnetic force field which will help the desire come to pass. Now we have a scientific basis for the age-old scriptural teaching that "As a man thinketh in his heart (thoughts) so is he."

Realize therefore that people who think about what they don't like in their lives, automatically create a magnetic force field to attract more of that which they do not like. Now is the time to learn how to plant thoughts and harvest the best. You are the Mental Gardener! My sister, Aleta Pearce Madsen shared with me the words in the Primary song book, *I Have A Garden,* p. G-18, which tells this concept well. The following is verse two:

I have a garden a secret garden
Where thot's like flowers grow day by day;
'Tis I must choose them, and tend and use them,
and cast all wrong ones like weeds away.
Goodness and love are seeds that I sow;
God up above will help me I know.
To keep my garden, my heart's own garden,
A place where beauty will always grow.

You Direct Your Own Thoughts

By Your Mental Effort
You Can Give Your Mind Commands Or
Dictate The Thoughts You Desire to Have.

This Emotional Body
Will Then Work To Match the Thought With A
Similar Emotion.

Positive Thoughts Trigger Endorphins, a natural positive body chemical, causing you to experience a natural high. You then feel happy and feel positive emotions. A JOY for life may truly be felt.

or

Negative Thoughts trigger a natural depressant giving you sad, negative emotions, allowing a depression cycle in your life.

- You Can State Your Hopes, Direct Your thoughts, and Become the Person You Desire to Become.

- Happiness Is Not an Accident
  It Is Something *You Decide To Become.*

- Because Your Positive Thoughts or Faith
  Are Tried Here On The Earth, Be On Guard Daily.

- To Be Able To Receive,
  Learn To Quickly Replace
  The Negative Thoughts With Your
  Positive *Hopes and Desires*

State: "I Know Jesus Christ Lives, and I Doubt Him Not"
Next Recite Your Confirmed Desires. – Ask for further
Light and Knowledge to guide you.

We Have Free Moral Agency

You Can Mentally Tell Negative, Doubting, Evil or Fearful Thoughts To Leave Your Mind By Mentally Filtering The Thought: "Will This Thought Improve the Quality of My Life?" (as quoted from Bob Proctor)

Then Thinking The Mental Command:
I Delete This "Thought" or
I Erase and Replace this Negative Idea or Thought.

Then Think The Thoughts That You Desire.
This Is "The Prayer In The Heart" Concept.

We Are To Serve With All Our: Hearts (thoughts &
emotions), Might, Mind and Strength.

Doubt Not In Your Heart, Your Thoughts!

Doubting or Unbelief Stops You From
Receiving Hidden Knowledge.

The scriptures express this idea to us in many places. James 4:3, 7-8 explains this very well.

3. Ye ask, and receive not, because ye ask amiss, . . .

7. Submit yourselves therefore to God. Resist the devil, and he will flee from you.

8. Draw nigh to God, and he will draw nigh to you. Cleanse your hands, ye sinners; and purify your hearts, *ye double minded.* -- James 4:3, 7-8

Here are some thoughts on what he is teaching us in the previous passage.

- Submit yourselves therefore to God = Pray unto Him always.
- Resist the devil = By your inner self-talk. He tries to spoil your life with negative, doubting, evil or fearful thoughts.
- And he will flee from you = Evil must always leave when we command it, because we have our moral agency. He cannot force anything against our will.
- Draw nigh to God, and he will draw night to you = Pray and He will answer. -- Mos. 24:10-17

- Cleanse your hands, ye sinners, and purify your hearts (thoughts) ye double-minded = Each of us need to become Single-minded.

But Their Minds Were Blinded By the god Of This World = Satan.

14. But their minds were blinded: for until this day remaineth the same veil untaken away in the reading of the old testament; which veil is done away in Christ.

15. But even unto this day, when Moses is read, the veil is upon their heart.

16. Nevertheless when it [our thoughts] shall turn to the Lord, the veil shall be taken away.
-- 2 Corinthians 3:14-16

3. But if our gospel be hid, it is hid to them that are lost:

4. In whom the god of this world [the spoiler] hath blinded the minds of them which believe not, lest the light of the glorious gospel of Christ, who is the image of God, should shine unto them.

6. For God, who commanded the light to shine out of darkness, hath shined in our hearts, . . .
-- 2 Corinthians 4:3-4, 6

The wicked are listening to their god of darkness, and The Pure In Heart are Spiritually Listening To Jesus Christ who shines into our Hearts.

Have Ye Inquired Of The Lord?

When Laman and Lemuel could not understand what their father had prophesied, Nephi answered them by saying: "Have ye inquired of the Lord?" --1 Nephi 15:8

...If ye will *not harden your hearts,* and ask me [the Lord] in faith, believing that ye shall receive, ...surely these things shall be made known unto you. -- 1 Nephi 15:11

Matthew 13:58 Gives Us Further Insight

58. And he did not many mighty works there because of their unbelief. -- Matthew 13:58 39

Even Jesus was not able to perform Miracles where there was unbelief. Can you see that it is our unbelief which stops Miracles from happening in your personal life or as Missionaries? You need to express your **Desires Unto the Lord,** and then expect Miracles after the Spirit has answered yes. Doubt not, for all things are possible unto the Lord and to those who believe in the power of Jesus Christ.

Knowledge Hidden Up Because Of Unbelief

13. Come unto me, O ye Gentiles, and I will show unto you the greater things, the knowledge which is **hid up because of unbelief.**

14. Come unto me, O ye house of Israel, and it shall be made manifest unto you how great things the Father hath laid up for you, from the foundation of the world; and it hath not come unto you, because of unbelief.

15. Behold, when ye shall rend that veil of unbelief which doth cause you to remain in your awful state of wickedness, and hardness of heart, and blindness of mind, then shall the great and marvelous things which have been hid up from the foundation of the world from you—yea, when ye shall call upon the Father in my name, with a broken heart [do to life's trials] and a contrite spirit [being teachable], then shall ye know that the Father hath remembered the covenant which he made unto your fathers, O house of Israel.

16. And then shall my revelations which I have caused to be written by my servant John be unfolded in the eyes of all people. -- Ether 4:13-16

The scriptures have been trying to help us awaken from our unbelief. Here are more scriptures showing us that we need to alter our Thoughts-Hearts.

Remember - He Whispereth In Their Ear
* Where do doubting, negative or fearful thoughts proceed from?

- How does the devil or Spoiler speak to us?
- 2 Nephi 28:22 explains that: "He whispereth in their ears."
20. For behold, at that day shall he [the 'Spoiler'] rage [be at war] in the hearts [in the Thoughts] of the children of men, and stir them up to anger against that which is good.

21. And others will he pacify, and lull them away into carnal security, that they will say: all is well in Zion; yea, Zion prospereth, all is well – and thus the devil cheateth their souls, and leadeth them away carefully down to hell.

22. And behold, others he flattereth away, and telleth them there is no hell: and he saith unto them: I am no devil, for there is none – and thus he whispereth in their ears, until he grasps them with his awful chains, from whence there is no deliverance.
-- 2 Nephi 28:20-22

Unbelief,
Hardness of Heart, Double-Mindedness,
These Are Things Which the Lord Deplores,
For They Can Destroy You and Me.

Each of Us Can Begin
To Understand Better What
Proverbs 23:17 Means.
"As a Man Thinketh in His *Heart,* So is He."

The Lost Books of the Bible have a great deal to say about doubting and double-mindedness and its effect in our lives. We will quote from 2 Hermes 9:1-11, taken from the Pseudepigrapha, published in 1911.

The Lost Books of The Bible.
    Remove from thee all doubting;
    And question nothing at all,
      when thou asketh anything of the Lord;
    Saying within thyself: how shall I be able to
      ask anything of the Lord and receive it,
    Seeing I have so greatly sinned against him?

    Do not think thus, but turn unto the Lord with
      all thy heart, [thoughts and feelings] *
    And ask of him without doubting. . .
    Wherefore purify thy heart [thoughts] from
      all the vices of this present world;

And thou shalt receive whatsoever good
   things thou shalt ask,

And nothing shall be wanting unto thee of all
   thy petitions:
If thou shalt ask of the Lord *without*
doubting . . .

But they that are not such shall obtain none
   of those things which they shall ask,
For they that are full of faith ask all things
   with confidence and receive from the Lord
Because they ask without doubting. . .

Wherefore, purify the heart from doubting,
And put on faith, and trust in God, *and thou*
   shalt receive all that thou shalt ask.
   But if thou shouldest chance to ask somewhat and
   not (immediately) receive it,
      Yet do not therefore doubt, because thou hast not
   presently received the petition of thy soul ...

But do not leave off to ask, and then thou shalt
   receive . . .

Else if thou shalt cease to ask, thou must complain
   of thyself, and not of God,

That he has not given unto thee what thou
 didst desire.
Consider therefore this *doubting*, how cruel
and pernicious it is;
And how it utterly roots out many from the faith,
 who were very faithful and firm.
For this doubting is the daughter of the devil, and
 deals very wickedly with the servants of God.

Despise it, therefore, and thou shalt rule
over it on every occasion.
Put on a firm and powerful faith;
For faith promises all things and perfects all things.
But doubting will not believe that it shall
 obtain anything, by all that it can do.

Faith cometh from above, from God;
 and hath great power.
But doubting is an earthly spirit, and
procedeth from the devil,
And has no strength.

Do thou therefore keep the virtue of faith,
And depart from doubting in which is no virtue
And thou shalt live unto God.--2 Hermas 9:1-11,

(*All emphasis with bold lettering, italics or brackets were
added by the author.)

The Lost Books of the Bible [Cleveland: World Publishing
Company, 1926], p. 221-22. Taken from the
Pseudepigrapha, published in 1911.

Evil Spirit Personages Can Whisper In Our Ear

My niece, Kerri Brinkerhoff Guthrie, had an enlightening experience in the MTC previous to her arrival in the Pittsburgh, Pennsylvania. Mission. The following is a letter Kerrie wrote to me dealing with 2 Nephi 28:22.

Dear Friends,

I truly believe that the experiences that we have in life are for our good to learn from. Some of these experiences should help us come closer to God our Heavenly Father and help us realize how closely connected the spiritual and physical worlds are. One such experience that I had at the MTC, in October of 1983, gave me more understanding of how spirit- to-spirit communication works. My experience happened as follows:

President Bishop at the MTC, gave us the understanding of the scripture in 2 Nephi chapter 28 verse 22. This scripture gave me more insight and a better understanding of how Satan and his co-helpers operate here on the earth.

The scripture states that "Satan whispereth in our ears." Literally in our mind and tries to bind us to the falsehoods spoken to us, that we might believe whatever they say about ourselves and others. These false ideas, if believed, can condition our actions through our thoughts.

As I lay in bed the next morning, the Lord lifted the veil from my eyes. The noise of the sisters in the next room, awoke me from a strange dream. And as I felt an impulse to open my eyes and get up, I felt another voice talking into my mind. It said, "Finish your dream – Relax – You don't need to be in any hurry – Stay in bed."

Then within a few seconds I realized that the ideas that were coming into my mind were not mine! (The key point is to be able to recognize the source of our thoughts and deal with them properly.)

The veil then lifted from my eyes and to the left of me, by my bed was a spirit personage whose mouth moved but I could only hear his ideas as they came into my mind as **thoughts and in my tone of voice.** I looked at him with curiosity feeling no fear. This spirit personage then recognized that I saw him and swiftly moved, disappearing through the wall.

I contemplated this experience and wrote it in my Journal. This experience taught me that, yes literally there are those who are around us who know us and want to deceive us and that even though we cannot always see them with our physical eyes, they are there. We must recognize and disagree with their messages. As we exert our faith in Christ and mentally cast out any thoughts that are impure, they can have no power over us. Joseph Smith has explained that they can have no more power over us than what we give to them. It is time for us to realize how the spiritual battles go on, in our minds or thoughts, so that we can be alert and overcome the evil one in our lifetime, to bind Satan for the Millennium. Moroni 7:12 helps us to understand:

12. Wherefore, all things which are good cometh of God; and that which is evil cometh of the devil; for the devil is an enemy unto God, and fighteth against him continually, and inviteth and enticeth to sin, and to do that which is evil continually.

Sincerely, Kerri Brinkerhoff

As you can see, this earth life is a very real test to which we must awaken.

PUZZLE PIECE #5
Listen To The Spirit

Carolyn P. Ringger

Listen To The Spirit

More on Spiritual Communication
Listening To The Spirit

PART I

- How Does God Speak To You?
- How Do You Hear It?
- What Should You Do About It?

Here is a little statement I heard somewhere, which I feel most aptly expresses this matter of communication with the Lord:

When you pray, you communicate with the Lord.

When you study the scriptures,
He communicates with you.

Listen- Spiritual Communication

We will consider in this lesson the very important matter of Spiritual Communication, what it is and how we may receive spiritual communication from God and resist the "Sinspiration" from the Spoiler.

We know from previous lesson material that there are two forces in the world, the force of good, which comes to us from God, and the force of evil, which comes to us from the powers of darkness. We know that these are very real forces and that we are able to receive from either one or the other or both. We also know that being double-minded means that we are not attuning ourselves to the directing influence of God, but are allowing ourselves to be distracted and be sidetracked by the forces of evil and the things of the world.

In the spirit world in the beginning, we were given our free agency, to choose for ourselves how we would live our lives. There was a great battle in heaven over this very issue. Rev. 12:7-9 explains this best:

> 7. And there was war in heaven: Michael and his angels fought against the dragon; and the dragon fought and his angels,

> 8. And prevailed not; neither was their place found any more in heaven.

> 9. And the great dragon was cast out, that old serpent, called the Devil, and Satan, which deceiveth the whole world: he was cast out into the earth, and his angels were cast out with him. -- Rev. 12:7-9

Modern revelation gives us insight as to what was the cause of this war. It was being fought over our free agency. Satan came before God demanding that he be given all power and he would see that all mankind was saved. D&C 29:36-40 tells about this war and this rebellion and how it affected us and our free agency.

36. And it came to pass that ... the devil was before Adam, for he rebelled against me, saying, Give me thine honor, which is my power; and also a third part of the hosts of heaven turned he away from me because of their agency.

37. And they were thrust down, and thus came the devil and his angels;

38. and behold, there is a place prepared for them from the beginning, which place is hell.

39. And it must needs be that the devil should tempt the children of men, or they could not be agents unto themselves; for if they never should have bitter they could not know the sweet –

40. Wherefore, it came to pass that the devil tempted Adam, and he partook of the forbidden fruit and transgressed the commandment, wherein he became subject to the will of the devil, because he yielded unto temptation. -- D&C 29: 36-38, 40

The following chart and scriptures further illustrate this struggle and choice we made in the pre-existence over our agency. It also shows the communication we are receiving from both of these forces.

Let Us Prove Them Herewith

As I taught my first class in February, 1982, the woman asked me, "Why do more negative thoughts come into my mind then positive thoughts?" I replied that this was a good question and my next concept, "Let Us Prove Them Herewith."

I like to fit all truths together. The more pieces of the puzzle I can fit together, the more understandable the picture becomes. I like to create a panorama-type perspective on life. I hope this picture will answer the above question for you as it has for me.

I hope this creates for you, a better understanding of life as to where we have come from and why we are here on earth. See these scriptural references; Revelation 12:4-7, Jude 1:6, Isaiah 14:12-16, Abraham 3:25-28, D & C 29:36-40.

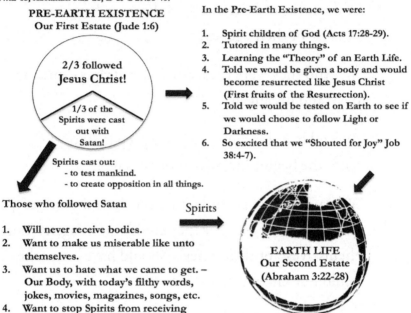

PRE-EARTH EXISTENCE
Our First Estate (Jude 1:6)

2/3 followed
Jesus Christ!

1/3 of the
Spirits were cast
out with
Satan!

Spirits cast out:
- to test mankind.
- to create opposition in all things.

In the Pre-Earth Existence, we were:

1. Spirit children of God (Acts 17:28-29).
2. Tutored in many things.
3. Learning the "Theory" of an Earth Life.
4. Told we would be given a body and would become resurrected like Jesus Christ (First fruits of the Resurrection).
5. Told we would be tested on Earth to see if we would choose to follow Light or Darkness.
6. So excited that we "Shouted for Joy" Job 38:4-7).

Those who followed Satan

Spirits

EARTH LIFE
Our Second Estate
(Abraham 3:22-28)

1. Will never receive bodies.
2. Want to make us miserable like unto themselves.
3. Want us to hate what we came to get. – Our Body, with today's filthy words, jokes, movies, magazines, songs, etc.
4. Want to stop Spirits from receiving bodies (abortion).
5. Want to destroy the family through divorce.
6. Evil has used masked messages in today's music to affect the minds of our youth.

As part of this Earth Life, we:

1. Receive a body.
2. Live by Faith and experience a "Living Laboratory."
3. Learn to make choices (keep the commandments).

After this earth life, all mankind will be resurrected. It is the free gift of the Savior to each of us. Now is the time for each of us to learn to turn life's negatives into positives and shout for joy because we are here!

The Negative Force Would Like You To Hate Your Body!

Realize that most curse words make fun of body parts, body functions or the way Babies are brought into this mortal world. Making and growing babies is very physical. These beings who will never have their own body want to help make us hate what we came to get, our body. Evil thoughts are projected to us. We are not evil in our real nature. We are spirit children of purified beings who are our heavenly parents.

Other words often used as curse words take the names of Deity in vain. Or they use "damn" and "hell", which describes the possible fate of many users of such words. Those impure beings (who make themselves so by their impure use of such terms) surely must not believe in the places or beings whose names they take in vain. People show little self-control when they use such terms which describe how they will be stopped in their own progression, and the way they will feel in that future hell. Then they will come to realize how they used their opportunity in this life and destroyed their own chances for progression. Earth life is not our beginning; it is our second estate and our time of probation in this Earth School. Here we are given the chance to choose, to see if we will learn to attune ourselves to the Pure Beings of Light and Truth, who care for this Universe, and are waiting there to receive us back.

How Does The Lord Speak To Us?

He says, "I stand at the Door and Knock."
His voice comes as Spirit speaking to Spirit, as a positive

impression, and from my own experience it comes most often in my own tone of voice because my mind is an instrument of my spirit.

I Stand At The Door And Knock

> 20. Behold, I stand at the door, and knock; if any man hear my voice, and open the door, I will come in to him, and will sup with him, and he with me.
> -- Rev. 3:20

Here is the Lord's invitation. He knocks, and seeks to come in unto us through His Spiritual Internet Server of inner positive, enlightening thoughts. But he cannot enter until we mentally attune ourselves, and open the door to receive him. His desire is to give us all things. But you and I can receive all things only as we open our hearts and minds to receive him. You ask for Light and Knowledge. His keys for opening the door is:

1. Pray and Ask questions,
2. Study,
3. Ponder in Faith
4. Ask – a question – then Listen
5. Use the gift of Discernment and Choose an Idea, then repeat steps one through five, as needed – round and around on the Faith Joy Cycle.

Yes, as you ask a question, then ponder, listen to the Still Small Voice, study, and continue to ask in Faith. You may receive influence of God in your heart, mind, and soul. It is most important that you have a prayer in your Heart as you ponder upon those things you have **asked** to understand, then answers may be reveled. Personal Revelation is a gift to all who will listen and attune themselves to the inner spiritual radio-like station from the Lord. So precious.

When ideas or thoughts come into your mind, ask yourself; are these thoughts positive, pure, and enlightening? Did I learn something new from them? Will this idea improve the quality of my life as I choose to follow Jesus Christ?

If the answer is yes, then you have received personal inspiration or revelation from the Lord – from the **Beings of Light** and **Truth**. It is part of our mission here on earth, to learn to become of one mind and one heart with these great resurrected Beings; God the Eternal Father, and His Son, Jesus Christ, (our elder brother), and with the Holy Ghost, yet a personage of Spirit. All that they have, you and I will be given. But we must be found **Pure In Thought** and learn to live the "Great Plan of Happiness," mentioned in Alma 42:8, 16, which is the Gospel of Jesus Christ.

Receiving And Recognizing Personal Revelation The Voice Of The Spirit

The Lord has often made reference to "The Voice of My Spirit" through which He gives us personal revelation. This voice is more often felt than heard. President Spencer W. Kimball, in explaining it pointed out that by always expecting the spectacular, many may miss entirely the constant flow of revealed communication." (Church News, 5 Jan. 1974, p. 2)

Elder S. Dilworth Young offers a most simple and beautiful explanation on receiving personal revelation. Said

he; "... Then as needed, according to his wisdom, his word will come into my mind through my thoughts, accompanied by a feeling ... of peace, a further witness that what one heard is right." He continues explaining that after we learn to recognize this feeling, this peace, we need never be drawn astray in our daily lives as guidance is received. We can also know that our personal revelation will always be in harmony with revealed principles. "It is vital for all of us to know also, that no one will ever receive revelation that is contrary to the living prophet."
-- S. Dilworth Young, Conference Report, April 1976, p. 34; or Ensign, May 1976, p. 23.

Hearing and recognizing the still small voice is also discussed in the Relief Society manual for 1984, under Visiting Teacher Messages, p. 8. This shows how the Lord taught Oliver Cowdery to receive revelation. The Lord explains this in the Doctrine and Covenants as follows:

> 6. Behold, thou knowest that thou hast inquired of me and I did enlighten thy mind, and now I tell thee these things that thou mayest know that thou hast been enlightened by the Spirit of truth. -- D&C 6:15

Another revelation was also given to Oliver Cowdery about the same time regarding this as follows:

> 2. Yea, behold, I will tell you in your mind and in your heart, by the Holy Ghost, which shall come upon you and which shall dwell in your heart,

> 3. Now behold, this is the spirit of revelation; . . .

4. Therefore this is thy gift; apply unto it, and blessed art thou, . . . -- D&C 8:2-4

We often refer to this form of revelation in the mind and in the heart as the "Still Small Voice", and there are a number of times when it is mentioned in the scriptures. Elijah referred to it in 1 Kings 19:12 and Nephi spoke of it in 1 Nephi 17:45. Helaman 5:30 refers to this "Still Small Voice" as does also D&C 85:6, which refers to "the still small voice, which whispereth through and pierceth all things..." D&C 88:66 explains ..."that which you hear is as the voice of one crying in the wilderness – in the wilderness, because you cannot see him – my voice, because my voice is Spirit; ..."

How may we recognize and receive this still small voice? Oliver Cowdery offered three steps which he used in his own life:

1. Search the scriptures
2. Keep the commandments
3. Ask in faith
    --Quoted in New Era, June 1980, p. 50

Therefore we were given our free agency, with the instructions to: "Prove all things; hold to that which is good." You were also instructed to pray always and to seek for knowledge, that you might be given promptings as to what is right for you. But in order to do this you must be willing to open your mind and heart and listen to His promptings.

Prove All Things; Hold Fast That Which Is Good

--1 Thess. 5:21

We were given this mortal life in which to study and choose the course which we will pursue. There are a number of scriptures which talk about this choice, wherin you are to prove all things for yourself. But the Lord has given us to understand that *we* are also being proved in this mortal probation. Abraham 3:25 is perhaps one of the best known quotations in this regard. During the Council in Heaven, God said that He would go down and He would make an earth whereon we may dwell; And that He would prove us herewith, to see if we will do all things whatsoever the Lord shall command. -- Abraham 3:25

Other scriptures include: D&C 98:14; "I will prove you in all things." And Exodus 16:4 and Deuteronomy 13:3. D&C 98:14 states that "... I have decreed in my heart, saith the Lord, that I will prove you in all things, whether you will abide in my covenants, even unto death, that you may be found worthy."

This earth life then, is a testing time for us, to help us make the right decisions. Thus it is vital that we learn to take advantage of the spiritual communication which the Lord has given us, that we may be guided by the Spirit so we will make the right decisions.

All of Earth Life is a huge school, and our daily challenges are our homework. Growth comes as the result of us learning how to work by **Faith** through our challenges. But we are not alone. It is time to attune each thought with the Lord's through the Still Small Voice.

The chart on the next page, *We Are A Living Internet Browser,* shows us how we actually receive from these web sites; either the Positive Station of Light and Knowledge or Inspiration, or the negative station of darkness and Sinspiration. We are choosing one or the other, for "No man can serve two masters; for either he will hate the one and love the other, or else he will hold to the one and despise the other. Ye cannot serve God and Mammon." (3 Nephi 13:24; Luke 16:13)

We really are a live Internet Browser, directed either to the web site of Light and Truth from God, or to Darkness and Sin from Satan, the Spoiler. It is ours to choose, experience after experience, until it is love we choose.

We Are Like Living Web Browsers

When we pull up this web site, the web site leads us into Darkness and it is difficult to see the pathway of life. It is blocked.

When we pull up this web site, the web site guides us and Lights our pathway in life.

Our Thoughts are Live Electrical Energy!

Negative, Doubting, Evil or Fearful. Thought is Sinspiration from the Spoiler

Light and Knowledge or Inspiration from God

- Always putting itself on top..
- Like an unwanted "pop up" web site.
- Mad feelings, provides links to click to take you to more and more unwanted web sites.

- The Light of Christ is unto all.
- Must ask to find the web site.
- Positive input and feelings.

Are we being 'Double Minded'?

"Erase"

3 Nephi 13:24

No man can serve two masters; for either he will hate the one, and love the other; or else he will hold to the one, and despise the other. You cannot serve God and mammon.

Enos' Experience

Enos explains how the Lord speaks to us; He says: "The voice of the Lord came into my mind." This and similar passages are repeated many times in the scriptures. All tell about how the voice of the Lord speaks to our spirit. Or it speaks as "the voice of the spirit", or as "the still small voice".

The Voice Of The Lord Came Into My Mind

10. And while I was thus struggling in the spirit, behold the voice of the Lord came into my mind again, ... -- Enos 1:10

The Voice Of The Spirit

11. And the Spirit said unto me again: Behold the Lord hath delivered him into thy hands ...

18. Therefore I did obey the voice of the Spirit ... --1 Nephi 4:11, 18

1. Verily, verily, I say unto you, I who speak even by the voice of my Spirit, even Alpha and Omega, your Lord and your God ... -- D&C 75:1

The Still Small Voice, Which Whispereth Through And Pierceth All Things

6. Yea, thus saith the still small voice, which whispereth through and pierceth all things, and often times it maketh my bones to quake while it maketh manifest, ... -- D&C 85:6

5. And it came to pass when they heard this voice, and beheld that it was not a voice of thunder, neither was it a voice of great tumultuous noise, but behold, it was a still voice of perfect mildness, as if it had been a whisper, and it did pierce even to the very soul ...
--Helaman 5:30

How Do We Communicate With The Lord?

At the beginning of this section we quoted a little statement that went like this:

- When we pray we communicate with the Lord.
- When we study the scriptures He communicates with us.
- We can see that it is through enlightening Thoughts to our mind.

The Lord tells us that we are to pray. Pray for or ask for that which we desire and which we feel is needful for our well being. The Lord asks that we study it out in our hearts and then ask Him. And He has promised us that if it be right, that we shall be blessed and receive it.

It need not even be a spoken hope or desire, but mentally sent by our thoughts. The Lord can hear it even if it is only within the chambers of our hearts, offered to Him when we cannot speak aloud. The story of the people of Alma, in Mosiah 24, tells how they were being persecuted by the wicked priest, Amulon, and were not even allowed to pray vocally. Yet they continued to pray unto God in their hearts (thoughts).

12. And Alma and his people did not raise their voices to the Lord their God, but did pour out their hearts to him; and he did know the thoughts of their hearts.
--Mosiah 24:12

What does it mean to study it out in your mind? This very important step is sometimes misunderstood or overlooked. Yet you cannot expect to receive from the Lord until you yourself have studied it out in your own mind, and know what it is that you want.

Study It Out In Your Mind And Heart Then Ask If It Be Right

How do you approach the Lord to ask for fulfillment of your righteous desires? When you pray to ask for Light and Knowledge, is that all that is required, or is there something further which is necessary in order to get your answers from God? This has been a subject which has occupied the people of God since the time of the creation, and in fact was one of the questions asked of Christ by his apostles shortly before his death. "Lord, teach us how to pray." *Teach us how to ask for the things that we desire, and to know they are right.*

An excellent answer to this question has been given us in modern revelation. Oliver Cowdery had been helping the Prophet Joseph Smith with the translation of the Book of Mormon. He began to desire to also do some translating, so he asked the Prophet, who inquired of the Lord, and Oliver was granted this privilege. However, he didn't understand what was required in order to exercise this gift, and it was taken away from him. Then in D & C 9:7-9, the Lord explained to him why his righteous desires were not fulfilled;

7. Behold you have not understood; you have supposed that I would give it unto you when you took no thought save it was to ask me.

8. But behold, I say unto you, that you must study it out in your mind; then you must ask me if it be right, and if it is right, I will cause that your bosom shall burn within you; therefore you shall feel that it is right.

9. But if it be not right you shall have no such feelings, but you shall have a stupor of thought ... --D&C 9:7-9

"You must study it out in your mind; then you must ask me if it be right." The Brother of Jared understood what he must do in order to receive answers from the Lord. Remember, in Ether 2:19 and 22, he asked the Lord for light for the vessels which he had built. He said: "I have done as thou hast commanded me; and I have prepared the vessels for my people, and behold there is no light in them. Behold, O Lord, wilt thou suffer that we shall cross this great water in darkness?" –Ether 2:22

The Lord's answer was significant. He said, "What will ye that I should do that ye may have light in your vessels?" (Ether 2:23) and he explained that they couldn't have windows or try to take fire in their vessels.

The Brother of Jared went up into the mountain and no doubt he did some studying and pondering of these things in his heart. Then, the scripture tells us, he "did molten out of a rock sixteen small stones; and they were white and clear, even as transparent as glass; and he did carry them in his hands upon the top of the mount, and cried again unto the Lord, saying:

... "O Lord, thou hast given us a commandment that we must call upon thee, that from thee we may receive according to our desires," ... And I know, O Lord, that thou hast all power, and can do whatsoever thou wilt for the benefit of man; therefore touch these stones, O Lord, with thy finger, and prepare them that they may shine forth in darkness ... that we may have light while we shall cross the sea." And the Lord did stretch out his hand and touched the stones to give them light. (Ether 3:2, 4, see also Ether 2:16-25 and 3:1-6 for the whole story)

The Brother of Jared studied it out in his heart then went to the Lord with a specific request.

There Are Many Voices Calling To Us

[There are many voices calling to us in this life, and much of this action occurs within our own minds. In fact,] "life's greatest battles are fought within the silent chambers of the mind." -- David O. McKay

I have come across many vivid experiences which opened

up to my understanding a vision of how these mental battles occur, the wrestling within of good vs. bad, of Inspiration vs. Sinspiration. The following experience revealed to me that a spirit may indeed speak to a mortal, though it is perceived as a thought or impression to the mind. *It is most often heard in the person's own tone of voice.* That person may then exercise his own free agency as to what he will do with that thought, whether he will accept or reject it.

Life Restored Through Inspiration Of The Spirit -- by Elder Edward J. Wood

Probably the most remarkable experience of Elder Wood's first mission resulted from a missionary's disobedience to his mother's council.

When Brigham Smoot left for his mission to Samoa he promised his Mother that he would not go in swimming as he did not know how to swim. However, since this was the only method of bathing in general use, his companion soon persuaded him to go in to bathe at sea with them. As the new Elder was wading out to sea, he slipped and fell into a deep hole in the reef. As he was unable to swim, he soon dropped to the bottom of the hole. Elder Wood had promised to be responsible for the new Elder's safety, and noticing him absent, began a frantic search. Brigham Smoot was soon found in the attitude of prayer at the bottom of the hole. His limp body was dragged from the hole and carried to the beach. Blood was flowing from his eyes, nose and mouth.

Elder Wood said of his companion, 'He was perfectly lifeless and dead,' In vain the Elders used all normal restorative measures.

By this time a large crowd of inquisitive natives had gathered around. Their telling about a native boy who had previously drowned in the same hole brought no comfort to the worried missionaries.

Elder Wood said that at this time, *he felt inspired by the Spirit,* that the only way his companion's spirit could re-enter his body would be to administer to him. Accordingly, the Body of Elder Smoot was dressed in clean garments with a new suit of clothes. The superstitious natives warned against such treatment of the body, and thought it sacrilegious to tamper with life and death.

Obedient to the inspiration, however, they anointed his head with oil (See James 5:14). While Elder Wood was sealing the anointing, he felt life come back into Elder Smoot's body. Shortly after the administration, Elder Smoot talked with the missionaries and bore solemn testimony to them. *He told of how,* in the spirit, he watched them recover his body from the hole, take it to the beach and try to restore it to life. He also told of touching Elder Wood on the shoulder and telling him that the only way to bring life back into the body was to use the Priesthood which he bore.

(Taken from SAMOAN MISSION JOURNAL, dated June 18, 1889 with Joseph Dean, President. Now in the Church Historian's office, Salt Lake City, Utah.)

This experience revealed to me that a spirit may speak to a mortal. It is perceived as a thought or *an impression to the mind,* and is heard in the mortal's own tone of voice. The Receiver, on his own free agency, then decides what to do with the thought.

Review – "How Does The Spirit Speak To You"?

There are a number of ways in which the Spirit can speak to your mind and heart and spirit. I should like to point them out, since it is very possible that, like the Lamanites spoken of in 3 Nephi 9:20, you may have experienced the whisperings of the Spirit and not even been aware that you did.

An article titled *Have I Received An Answer From The Spirit?*, printed in the Ensign, April 1989 (p 21-25) lists a number of these ways in which you may have been prompted by the Spirit. I urge you to get that article and read it, since it offers several vivid illustrations. It is important to be able to recognize the Spirit when you receive it. Here then are the ways that are mentioned:

The Spirit Speaks Peace To The Mind – This is one of the most common manifestations of the Spirit. Feelings such as calmness, peace and tranquility. D&C 6:23 speaks of this. Here Oliver Cowdery was seeking for a witness from the Lord during the time of the translation of the Book of Mormon. The Lord tells him, "Did I not speak peace to your mind concerning the matter? What greater witness can you have than from God?"

The Spirit Causes Your Bosom or Inner Soul To Burn – Perhaps you have experienced this tingling feeling during an inspirational Sacrament meeting, as I have, or just before you felt called to get up and bear your testimony. This is spoken of in D&C 9:8, "...and if it is right I will cause that your bosom shall burn within you; therefore you shall feel that it is right."

Here is an experience when I have felt the burning within me:

When giving a Book of Mormon away using Elder Hartmon Rector Jr.'s idea of asking people if they like to read. When they said yes, I offered to give them a copy of a wonderful book telling about the visit of Jesus Christ to the Americas and asked would they like to read about it if I sent them a copy? They wrote their name and address on a card for me.

When the Missionaries delivered the book, they presented the card that the person had filled out, quickly creating a comfort zone. Now the Missionaries could tell them more about the Book of Mormon and perhaps have a contact.

The family who received our Book of Mormon was baptized on June 3, 1989, and we were invited to the Gilbert Stapley Stake Center to witness the baptism. The husband was baptized first and ordained a Priest so he could baptize his wife. As she was being baptized, I felt the sweet tingling presence of the spirit of the Holy Ghost sweep over my body. How the Spirit works with us is marvelous indeed.

The Spirit Tells You In Your Mind and Your Heart – When the Holy Ghost speaks, your mind may be struck with insight and clarity and you have a sudden understanding of the meaning of that passage or that doctrine. Or it may be simply a feeling, "Yes, that makes sense." Now I understand what that means.

The answer was given me as I pondered on *how* we will bind Satan. I was walking across the kitchen when the answer flashed into my Mind. I believe it will be in part, because we will listen to him no more in our *hearts,* our *thoughts!*

I remember standing there in the middle of the room amazed at what I was seeing with my mind's eye. I wondered at the time, "Would anybody believe me if I told them what I can see? *I saw with my mind's eye that we can learn to bind Satan!*" My whole body was filled with JOY at that moment.

Can you imagine the JOY that I felt later when I was given a chance to share this marvelous concept with others in the Mesa 18th Ward newspaper. The experience was also reprinted in the Mesa 30th Ward newsletter, within the same month.

The Spirit Comes As A Voice In The Mind – I have had a number of such experiences where I heard the Voice of the Spirit speaking to me, directing what I should do.

1. We Need To Get Away To a Cabin – page 236
2. Our Green Plants –page 240
3. Send the Children to Utah –page 239
4. Elder Woods, –*Life Restored through Inspiration Of The Spirit.* - Page129
5. Mt. Vernon, "Yes My Daughter, You Are Doing What I Desire of You" – page 248

The Spirit Leads – At no time will the Spoiler lead someone to do good. This is expressed in Moroni 7:17, "...he persuadeth no man to do good, no not one ..." and Hyrum Smith in the D&C 11:12 was told, "... put your trust in that Spirit which leadeth to do good, yea, to do justly, to walk humbly, to judge righteously, and this is my Spirit."

The Spirit Occupies Your Mind and Presses Upon Your Feelings - A vivid illustration of this is recorded in D&C 128:1 where Joseph Smith, in an epistle to the church expressed his concerns about baptism for the dead. He said, " ...I now resume the subject of baptism for the dead, as that subject seems to occupy my mind and press itself upon my feelings the strongest..."

The Spirit Constrains – to restrain or warn against. There are many recorded instances where a person felt an inner warning against pursuing a certain course. They heeded this voice and avoided some disaster, or were made to know that pursuing that course would be against the Lord's wishes. Alma 14:11 gives an illustration of this where Alma tells Amulek; ..."the spirit constraineth me that I must not stretch forth mine hand." (to save believers from the flames)

Joseph Smith, in a visit to Brigham Young after his martyrdom, commented on the importance of paying heed to the still small voice and directed him to tell the people to be careful not to turn from the direction of the Spirit. But in order to heed this voice most fully we must understand what is the voice of the Spirit, and be attuned to receiving it, and recognize that many times it is there guiding and directing us, even sometimes when we may not have been aware of it. So as you study, ponder and pray, by asking for further Light and

Knowledge keep this in mind, and be open to the direction which the Spirit can offer.

The Ten Steps Of Faith – Or –
The Faith-Joy Cycle

Through faith we may receive all things, and be inspired on how to solve each of your problems. And as we do, we will grow and find greater happiness and joy. That is what I feel the Lord intended when he told us; "Men are that they might have joy." –2 Nephi 2:25

As I have taught classes over the past years, I have come to understand more and more clearly what the Ten Steps of Faith are in the Faith-Joy Cycle, and how to use them. I will share the steps I followed below. As you study, them note how each of these elements build on and support the next.

1. You have a Problem or a CHALLENGE.
2. THINK how you Hope or Desire to solve the Challenge. Ether 3:2
3. Ask: "Is this Desire for my good?" Confirm it by the Spirit. D&C 46:7-9, 23, 30
4. When the Spirit says yes – (Correct until you receive a Yes.)
5. Your Desire becomes God's will for you by asking in the Spirit. "Wherefore it is done even as he asketh." D&C 46:30
6. Ask for your confirmed desire and DOUBT NOT-- Mormon9:18-21 --Alma 56:47-8, 57:26 --Moroni 7:25 --D&C 67:1-3
7. Weary the Lord until He blesses you with your confirmed desire. Luke 18:1-8
8. Receive the MIRACLE! --Mormon 9:21
9. FEEL JOY!
10. GIVE THANKS!

FULFILLMENT AND JOY, these are the side effects of living our lives by the LAWS OF FAITH. This Faith-Joy Cycle may be repeated as often as is needed, as you approach the Lord about fulfillment of each of your needs and desires.

Spiritual Communication

Part II

More On How Satan "The Spoiler" Works

- The Devil works by Putting Negative, Doubting or Evil thoughts Into Your Mind and in your own tone of voice – sort of. Then pushes against you, saying – "Look at YOUR Thoughts, you are an evil person." Etc.
- His goal is to Spoil your life.
- The word, Devil, in Greek means Slanderer, Demon, Adversary
- In Hebrew the word devil means "Spoiler" – The term "Spoiler" describes him well. The evil one does not try to satan your joy, nor devil your joy. His Goal is to - Spoil Your Joy.

The LDS Bible Dictionary p. 656 offers further information regarding the devil and how he works. It points out that the devil is the enemy of righteousness and of those who seek to do the will of God. Literally, a spirit son of God, he was at one time an angel in authority in the presence of God; however, he rebelled in the premortal life, at which time he persuaded a third of the spirit children of the Father to rebel with him, in opposition to the plan of salvation championed by Jehovah (Jesus Christ). "Thus came the devil and his angels" (D&C 29:37). They were cast out of heaven and were denied the experience of mortal bodies and earth life. Latter-day revelation confirms the Biblical teaching that the devil is a reality and that his focus is to lead men and women from the work of God. One of the major techniques of the devil is to cause human beings to think they are following God's ways, when in reality they are deceived by the devil to follow other paths.

He is miserable in his situation, and "stirreth up the children of men unto secret combinations of murder and all manner of secret works of darkness," and tries to imitate the works of God.

How Does The Spoiler Speak To You?

How does Satan work to spoil your life?

We will now consider the negative element of communication, and how Satan works to spoil and destroy our lives. Both the voice of good and the voice of evil are around us all the time. We must be tuned in to receive the inspiration from God, but the "sinspiration" from the Spoiler is always there, blaring at us from every direction. And his voice is very subtle and very cunning, so much so that we must always be on our guard so that we don't let Satan sneak upon us, while we are unaware.

He is always there blaring at us from the voices of the world, including music lyrics, advertisements, TV, magazines, email and Internet sites. But he can also creep in and seek to overcome us from within. The voice of doubt, of fear, of anger, envy, pride, and greed all are the voices of Satan, and we must recognize them as such, and build up our armor against him. First learn to recognize the thoughts are from Satan. Delete the attacking thoughts and put on your mental armor from God.

Spirit Can Speak To Your Spirit

You receive spiritual information in the form of a thought or an idea and most often in your own tone of voice. Satan's most potent weapon is through your thoughts. He may put into your mind the following: "You're no good, remember when you _____ . Or "You can't get a better job, so why try?" Or "You're fat and ugly. Nobody wants you for a friend." He can even project an immoral thought into your mind then continue by accusing you of being the creator of the thought. He says: "Look at what you're thinking. You're a hypocrite. What makes you think you're such a good Latter-Day Saint/Christian (or whatever religion you may be)? If your friends at church knew what you are thinking about, they wouldn't want to be your friend."

In this way he whispers in your ear to make you react through the body's emotions. To Our sons might come... "You are not worthy to pass the Sacrament." You may feel depressed or angry or fearful or guilty, and unless you take immediate firm action to root out these negative thoughts and command them to leave, or you might end up believing them. He does his work well. You and I have bought his whole package, at hurtful times in our lives and accepted it as our own, all in error to our real self.

Learning To Discern, Is A Gift Of The Spirit.
(See D&C 46:7-23)

Is This the Voice of the Spoiler?
You are now noticing, how he speaks to you in your own mind. Also, the negative is true in some way, making it so you

will accept the thoughts as your own. Notice too, how he always addresses you as "You". This is one way "You" can know when the whisperings are from Satan. When you speak to yourself about yourself, do you think of yourself as "You"? Of course not. You think of yourself as "I" and your self-talk is always thought and spoken in that way: "I will do this," or "I like that". So this is one way you can know that these whisperings are from the Spoiler.

Another way you can know is how you feel about yourself and the world. Do your thoughts leave you feeling good and uplifted? Or do they leave you feeling angry and depressed? If they are negative and destructive, you can know that they are from the spoiler's system of internal whispering. They are not your thoughts and you can command them to leave. You can "Erase and Replace" or say *I erase this thought!* Get rid of the negative thoughts and replace them with constructive and uplifting positive thoughts. Ask, does this thought improve the quality of my life? Remember that to erase a negative thought just takes Mental Effort.

Erasing Negative Thoughts

By your mental efforts you can give your mind commands, and dictate the thoughts that you desire to have. We all have agency, and you can tell your negative, doubting, evil thoughts, or unjustified fears to leave. You then can think the thoughts that you desire, by calling upon God to help you overcome this evil influence.

James explains that if you ask and receive not, it is because you ask amiss. Let us refer back to this scripture.

> 3. Ye ask and receive not, because ye ask amiss . . .
>
> 7. Submit yourselves therefore to God. Resist the devil and he will flee from you.
>
> 8. Draw nigh to God, and he will draw nigh to you. Cleanse your hands, ye sinners; and purify your hearts, ye double minded. -- James 4:3, 7-8

I would like to offer just a few personal thoughts on this scripture. "Submit yourselves therefore to God (pray in humility and openness of spirit). Resist the devil (who spoils our lives through negative, doubting, or evil thoughts), and he will flee from you. (**Evil must leave when you command it to because you have agency** and he cannot force anything upon you. If you resist him, there will be no dwelling place for him). Draw nigh to God, and he will draw nigh to you. Cleanse your hands, ye sinners, and purify your hearts (or your thoughts), ye double minded. –James 4:8 The Spirit would have us become Single-Minded.

On this and the following pages we will consider some of the things the scriptures have to say about the workings of Satan. He is doing these things now and he has always worked in this manner to hurt and destroy the children of men.

Lying Sent Forth By Satan To Harden Their Hearts

> 22. And it came to pass that from this time forth there began to be lyings sent forth among the people, by Satan, to harden their hearts, to the intent that they might not believe in those signs and wonders which

they had seen; but notwithstanding these lyings and deceiving the more part of the people did believe, and were converted unto the Lord. --3 Nephi 1:22

Hard In Their Hearts, Imagining Some Vain Thing

1. And it came to pass that thus passed away the ninety and fifth year also, and the people began to forget those signs and wonders which they had heard, and began to be less and less astonished at a sign or a wonder from heaven, insomuch that they began to be hard in their hearts, and blind in their minds, and began to disbelieve all which they had heard and seen...

2. Imagining up some vain thing in their hearts, that it was wrought by men and by the power of the devil, to lead away and deceive the hearts of the people; and thus did Satan get possession of the hearts of the people again, insomuch that he did blind their eyes and lead them away to believe that the doctrine of Christ was a foolish and vain thing. --3 Nephi 2:1-2

Satan Hath Put It Into Their Hearts

10. And, behold, Satan hath put it into their hearts to alter the words which you have caused to be written, or which you have translated, which have gone out of your hands.

13. For he hath put into their hearts to do this, that by lying they may say they have caught you in the words which you have pretended to translate.

15. For behold, he has put it into their hearts to get thee to tempt the Lord thy God, in asking to translate it over again.

20. Verily, verily, I say unto you, that Satan has great hold upon their hearts; he stirreth them up to iniquity against that which is good;

32. And, behold, they will publish this, and Satan will harden the hearts of the people to stir them up to anger against you, that they will not believe my words. -- D&C 10:10, 13, 15, 20, 32

Here is another example of how Satan works in the minds and hearts of the people in our day:

Lucifer Tries To Hinder Temple Work
By President Rudger Clawson

On one occasion I heard the late Apostle Marriner W. Merrill, President of the Logan Temple, relate this extraordinary incident:

He was sitting in his office one morning, he said, when he noticed from the window a company of people coming up the hill to the Temple. As they entered the Temple grounds they presented rather a strange appearance, not only in dress but in their mode of travel. Some were riding on horses, others were in conveyances, and still others were afoot. He wondered who they could be as he was not looking for a company of such size that particular morning. They dismounted from their horses, stepped down from their conveyances, put their animals under the shade and walked about complacently as if they had a perfect right to be there.

A little later a person unknown to Brother Merrill entered the room. Brother Merrill said to him: "Who are you and who are these people who have come up and taken possession of the Temple grounds unannounced?" He answered and said: "I am Satan and these are my people." Brother Merrill then said: "What do you want? Why have you come here?" Satan replied: "I don't like the work that is going on in this Temple and feel that it should be discontinued. Will you stop it?" Brother Merrill answered and said emphatically, "No, we will not stop it. The work must go on." "Since you refuse to stop it, I will tell you what I propose to do," the adversary said. "I will take these people, my followers, and distribute them throughout this Temple district, and will instruct them to whisper in the ears of people, persuading them not to go to the Temple, and thus bring about a cessation of your Temple work." Satan then withdrew.

President Merrill, commenting on this strange interview with the Evil One, said that for quite a period of time the spirit of indifference to Temple work seemed to take possession of the people and very few came to the House of the Lord. The presumption was that Satan had carried out his threat which caused a temporary lull in Temple work. It is not to be

wondered at that Satan, who is the enemy of all righteousness, is displeased with temple work. -- From the
--Church News December 12, 1936 Vol. 344, No. 61

Spiritual Communications . . .

An Overview and Summary

We are literally spiritual receiving sets; able to hear and respond to the voices from the spirit world. Always we have access to two voices, either to "Inspiration" from the spirit of God, or "Sinspiration" from the temptings of Satan and of the world. We are accountable for the choices we make. Satan tries in every way he can to tempt us and lead us astray, but we always have access to inspiration and help from God to lead us and guide us. We have that direction not only through the scriptures, but also through the voice of the Spirit, the promptings and guidance of the Holy Ghost. We need to attune our hearts to that counsel in order that we may grow and find peace and joy in our lives.

Alma has pointed out that we are accountable even for our thoughts. President Ezra Taft Benson explains that our accountability begins with how we handle the evil thought immediately after it is presented to us. Like Jesus we should promptly and positively terminate the temptation, and not allow the devil to elaborate, and beguile us with all his insidious reasoning. We should promptly and properly let it go, then immediately replace it with positive and uplifting thoughts in order not to allow that thought to return

Here are some points of review from this chapter:

- A Spirit can speak to our spirit.
- We receive it as a thought or idea in our minds, and most often in our own tone of voice.
- We must discern from whence the prompting comes. We can recognize it by the way it makes us feel. If it be from the evil one, we must immediately cast it out, that we may be better prepared to rule over the Spoiler on every occasion. This is part of the binding of Satan in preparation for the coming of the Millennium.

The Lord has given us one final sure proof, that we may know that we are indeed inspired of him.

Did I Not Speak Peace To Your Mind?
> 23. Did I not speak peace to your mind concerning the matter? What greater witness can you have than from God? -- D&C 6:23

Assignments:

1. Read the book: "There Is No Death," by Sarah LaNelle Menet. 2002
2. Read "Return From Tomorrow" by George Ritchie.

Puzzle Piece #6
Make A Miracle

Carolyn P. Ringger

Make A Miracle

How Do You Bring About A Miracle?

We as Humans see a miracle as being something beyond the ordinary course of nature, something brought about through the divine intervention of God. There have been miracles wrought from the very beginning through the power of God, and it has only been during times of apostasy and unbelief that miracles have ceased.

Faith precedes the miracle, and if there be no faith there can be no miracle. The scriptures tell us this over and over. Ether 12:12 states that:

> 12. If there be no faith among the children of men, God can do no miracle among them; wherefore he showed not himself until after their faith.
> --Ether 12:12

Miracles, then, happen as a result of our faith. And we can experience miracles only in answer to our righteous desires, which have been built upon faith, hope, and prayer.

How then may we make miracles happen in our own lives? Let us go over the following thoughts listed:

Faith Precedes
The Miracle!

Q: If Faith Precedes
The Miracle,
Then What
Precedes Faith?

A: Your Hopes or Desire.

Can you see now why. . .
If Ye Have No Hope
Ye Must Needs Be
In Despair!
--Moroni 10:22

Or have Feelings of 'Depression'

Faith Is What Creates All Miracles And Greatness In Each Of Our Lives.

The Apostle Paul tells us in Hebrews:

> 6. But without faith it is impossible to please him; for he that cometh to God must believe that he is, and that he is a rewarder of them that diligently seek him. - - Hebrews 11:6

We cannot Please God unless we have Faith? This scripture used to feel negative and unpleasant to me. Then I began to realize what it is that the scripture is really saying. And I began to understand better what the Lord *is asking of us*.

The Lord of all is waiting to help us. He wants to help us – if we will let him. But that means that we must know what it is we Desire and be able to ask for it specifically. Doubting Nothing.

"What will ye that I shall do for you?" the Lord asked the Brother of Jared (Ether 2:23 and 25). The Brother of Jared was able to ask specifically for what was needed, because he had studied out his challenge in his heart and had reached a solution and then proceeded to ask the Lord if it was correct.

The Lord can only help us as we Ask and Doubt Not, which equals Faith! The Lord is pleased when we, by our Faith make it possible for Him to help us. Mormon 9:21 records for us the Right Way to ask and receive. We need to know HOW the God in whom we should trust works. If we receive nothing, we have unbelief or negative thoughts (Mormon 9:20), plus if we have fears in our hearts we can receive Nothing. Fear emotions and doubts stop the miracles from coming to us from the Lord. (D&C 67:1-3)

To keep these truths clear in your mind, remember that ...

... To Have Faith = You Believe In Jesus Christ
You Doubt Not That He Lives
And That He Can Do All Things!
Now, Keep Your Inner Self-Talk Positive
Over Your Desires,
Then You Shall Receive!

Each of us needs to learn to know that Jesus Christ Lives. You doubt Him not, then your righteous desires, confirmed by the Spirit, are the miracles which will come to pass due to your single-minded prayers of faith to the Lord. The Lord of all is pleased when we, by our faith, make it possible for Him to help us through our faith.

How Do You Make Miracles Happen In Your Life?

Here is a secret. You can actually have miracles happen in your life today. Through the miracle of faith you can catch a glimpse of and start to achieve that beautiful reward which the Lord holds in store for you, both here and hereafter. Then you can actually begin to experience that miracle, right here, right now. Through faith, lives are transformed and people come to experience a Joy they had never anticipated and never experienced before.

Can faith actually be that strong? Can it produce such a miracle in my life and yours? We read about it in the scriptures all the time, and we accept that. People in ages past, were normal human beings just as we are. So their experiencing of a miracle came about through obeying the laws of faith, just as it can and will for each of us as we put the laws of faith into practice in our lives.

I would like to cite a couple of instances as told in the Book of Mormon. The story of the sons of Mosiah and Alma the younger and what happened in their lives is a dramatic example of the power of faith, as is the story of the 2,000 stripling young warriors, who expressed and lived by the faith that their mothers had taught them.

Alma And Sons Of Mosiah

Alma the younger and the sons of Mosiah had been persecutors of the church and people of God, which caused great sorrow and pain to their fathers. Yet through the faith and prayers of Alma and Mosiah and others, their sons received a dramatic heavenly manifestation wherein an angel appeared to them and chastised them severely. As a result of this experience they turned their lives around, and dedicated their lives to missionary work thereafter.

The whole story of the missionary labors of the sons of Mosiah among the Lamanites is a beautiful story of great faith and works. Through their faith they were able to convert whole nations of the Lamanites, starting with Lamoni, king of one Lamanite nation, and his queen. And then later also the father of Lamoni, who was king over all seven kingdoms of the Lamanites. As a result the whole Lamanite nation, with the exception of some dissenters, joined the church of God.

They took a covenant at that time that they would never

again go to war with their brethren. The old king said, "Now my beloved brethren, since God hath taken away our stains, and our swords have become bright, then let us stain our swords no more with the blood of our brethren . . . as a testimony to our God." (Alma 24:12, 15)

The 2,000 Young Warriors

However, those who had remained outside the church sought then to take advantage of them, and the Nephites were forced to take up arms to defend their brethren for a time. Their sons, however, had not taken this oath, and they determined that they would go forth and defend their people from the marauders. These were the 2,000 stripling warriors who proved to be such an inspiration to their people. Alma 53:18-19 tells us:

> 18. Now behold, there were two thousand of those young men, who entered into this covenant and took their weapons of war to defend their country . . . And they would that Helaman should be their leader
> --Alma 53:18-19

Helaman In An Epistle Later To Moroni Says:

> 46. I had ever called them my sons (for they were all of them very young) even so they said unto me: Father, behold our God is with us, and he will not suffer that we should fall; then let us go forth . . .
>
> 47. Now they never had fought, yet they did not fear

death and they did think more upon the liberty of their fathers than they did upon their lives; yea, they had been taught by their mothers, that if they did not doubt, God would deliver them.

48. And they rehearsed unto me the words of their mothers, saying: We do not doubt our mothers knew it. -- Alma 56:46-48

55. And now it came to pass that when they (the Lamanites) had surrendered themselves up unto us, behold I numbered those young men who had fought with me, fearing lest there were many of them slain.

56. But behold, to my great joy, there had not one soul of them fallen to the earth; yea, and they had fought as if with the strength of God; ...
--Alma 56: 55-56

21. Yea, and they did obey and observe to perform every word of command with exactness; yea, and even according to their faith it was done unto them.

25. ... according to the goodness of God, and to our great astonishment, and also the joy of our whole army, there was not one soul of them who did perish; yea, and neither was there one soul among them who had not received many wounds.

26. And now, their preservation was astonishing to

our whole army, yea, that they should be spared while
there was a thousand of our brethren who were slain.
And we do justly ascribe it to the miraculous power of
God, because of their exceeding faith in that which
they had been taught to believe – that there was a just
God, and whosoever did not doubt that they should
be preserved by his marvelous power.
--Alma 57:21, 25-26

These 2,000 young warriors exercised total faith, and the
Lord blessed them accordingly. They had no doubts and they
had no fears. By contrast, the men in the next scripture
feared and allowed doubts to enter, and they were told that
this was the reason that they did not receive.

There Were Fears In Your Hearts

In order to receive you must ask in faith, nothing
doubting. A dramatic illustration of this came in the early
days of the restored church when some of the leading elders
had asked for a special blessing. That blessing was not
forthcoming, however, and the revelation in D&C 67:1-3
explains the reason why:

1. Behold and hearken, O ye elders of my church, who
have assembled yourselves together, whose prayers I
have heard, and whose hearts I know, and whose
desires have come up before me.

3. Ye endeavored to believe that ye should receive the
blessing which was offered unto you; but behold,

verily I say unto you that there were fears in your hearts, and verily this is the reason that ye did not receive. -- D&C 67:1, 3

The Lord told them that the reason they did not receive was that "there were fears in your hearts". By contrast, Mormon 9:21 expresses the promise which will be given us when we ask and doubt not:

> 21. Behold, I say unto you that whoso believeth in Christ, doubting nothing, whatsoever he shall ask the Father in the name of Christ it shall be granted him; and this promise is unto all, even unto the ends of the earth. --Mormon 9:21

How Miracles Will Come

Can thought produce a miracle? Consider the promise which the Lord has given us in Mormon 9:21: "Whatsoever he shall ask the Father in the name of Christ it shall be granted him..." then ponder and study out the method he has given us to achieve the miracle.

Elder Hartman Rector Jr. in his book, *Already To Harvest* (p. 44) tells us that "thoughts produce an effect as literal as physical exertion". It was by thought, you will remember, that the Lord first created the world and everything in it. "For I, the Lord God, created all things of which I have spoken, spiritually, before they were naturally upon the fact of the earth . . ." (Moses 3:5. See also v. 7, 9) Also the experience of Alma and the followers of Christ, in Mosiah 24:10-17 tells how they were delivered because the

Lord heard the prayer in their Hearts (their thoughts). It is always by thought and mental exertion first that we bring forth any creation. Lectures on Faith (p. 61 #3) reminds us that "when a man works by faith he works by mental exertion instead of physical force."

Here we literally have a spiritual internet service with the Beings of Light. They know our very thoughts. So using this spiritual communication in the Right Way, we can experience the fruits of our faith, or MIRACLES.

Said President Brigham Young:

> The greatest mystery a man ever learned is to know how to control the human mind and bring every faculty and power of the same in subjection to Jesus Christ; this is the greatest mystery we have to learn while in these tabernacles of clay.
>
> --Journal of Discourses 1:46

We were sent here to learn how to develop our spirit intelligence to the point of controlling our heart (thoughts). We have been taught to; "Seek Ye First The Kingdom of God and ALL things will be Added unto you." (Matthew 6:33 or 3 Nephi 13:33). We should exercise our faith over all our righteous desires.

Does that mean our small material affairs? Is that mundane daily problem, my house plants, that needed piece of furniture, that job, or that snarl in our household affairs worthy of the Lord's attention? The Lord says that it is. He tells us in Alma 37:37

> 37. Counsel with the Lord in all thy doings, and he
> will direct thee for good; yea, when thou liest down at

night lie down unto the Lord, that he may watch over you in your sleep; and when thou risest in the morning let thy heart be full of thanks unto God . . ."
-- Alma 37:37

He has told us to cry over our flocks and our fields and over everything that we do. (Alma 34:20-25. See also v. 17-18)

THOUGHT PRODUCES EFFECTS
A Formula Given Us By God

The Lord has given us a formula and means whereby we may, through faith, achieve all our righteous desires. It starts with the thought, the desire of our heart. Use the moments of the day, when you are not required to deal with other things mentally, to think on these things. Ponder them. Study them out in your heart. Focus on them, like a prayer in the heart all day. We need to think about our hopes and desires in order to have our eyes and intelligence single to the glory of God. And as they grow and take on strength, our faith will grow. It will become spontaneous as it takes on power and strength. Luke 18:1-8 tells us that we should weary the Lord until he blesses us. All things are possible to them that believeth. Inspiration will come into our minds by the Holy Ghost, and we must do as we are inspired.

Then will come the Miracle, which we have achieved through our Mental Effort our Faith.

Consider the following graph, which offers an outline on how we may go about it.

Thought Produces Effects

7. Give Thanks
6. The MIRACLE
5. Weary the Lord or Ask
4. Inspiration will come
3. Faith
2. Focus on Righteous Desires
1. Thought

YOUR   THE MIRACLE

1. Takes Mental exertion.
2. Like a prayer in the Heart all day.
3. Becomes spontaneous & will increase.
4. Do as inspired
5. Until He blesses you.
6. THE MIRACLE
7. Give Thanks!

Faith Is An Ever-Increasing Spiral . . .

Using Faith In Our Missionary Work

Write Down A Date

Apostle M. Russell Ballard taught about the principles of faith in his October 1984 conference address. He says:

> "May I suggest a simple way in which each one of us can exercise our faith and start our personal missionary service. Write down a date in the near future on which you will have someone ready to be taught the gospel. Do not worry that you do not have someone already in mind. Let the Lord help you as

you pray diligently for guidance. Fast and pray, seeking guidance and direction from our Heavenly Father."

Yes, the Lord will inspire us. How? The Holy Ghost will speak into our minds and inform us as we ask him. We need to purify the inner vessel to be ready when the Spirit whispers within our Heart (our Minds) the names of people, then follow through on the impression or desires we are given.

Apostle Ballard continues:

"Many, if not all, of you will have special spiritual experiences as the Lord inspires you. I know from my own personal and family missionary experience that the Lord will enlighten your mind. He will sharpen your vision of this work by bringing names of nonmembers to your mind that you have never before regarded as potential members of the Church. As you continue, you will be blessed to know what you should say and how you approach each person."

"Brothers and sisters, you will notice that I did not suggest that you write down a name, but rather that you write down a specific date. The key to our success will be to ask for divine guidance that we might be directed to those who will accept the gospel."

Realize that there is nothing too hard for the Lord. The problem is that we have Unbelief. Then we need to switch our Mental Gears to the Belief cycle. By our Mental Effort we can use our faith. We can present our desire to the Lord and weary the Lord until he blesses us with the Righteous Desires of our Hearts.

Faith And Miracles Today

We have cited two scriptural examples where faith preceded the miracle. Yet you may wonder, can it happen to me today? Here are a few examples of people today who are making use of the principles of faith, miracles, and joy as expressed through this Faith Unpuzzled Lesson Material.

Missionary Miracles

The following story is an account of how Sister Morgan and Sister Johnson of the Arizona, Tempe Mission, used the Laws of Faith to receive their righteous desires.

"We went through the Faith Unpuzzled material during the month of June 1989. As we focused on the principles of Faith in our missionary work, we saw miracles happen!

"At the beginning of the month, we prayerfully set our June goal for four baptisms. Although this was a high goal set for the area we were then serving in, we felt confident that with the Lord's help we would obtain it. Incidentally, when we set this goal, we had no investigators committed to be baptized that month.

"By the middle of the month, we had yet to see any progress in our area, and were facing discouragement and frustration. At this time, we started to learn these concepts on the "Laws of Faith" and how they could work for us. We began to place scriptures up all over our home. We especially focused on Mormon 9:18-21, D&C 46:7, 30 and Moroni 7:20-21, 25-26. These scriptures helped us to understand that our testimony of Christ was the foundation of our faith, and nothing is impossible for Him. We wrote up the things we desired in our work, and kept them continually in our minds, along with our testimonies of Jesus Christ. We also mentioned these desires in all of our personal and companion prayers.

We soon discovered that this was not all there was to reaching our desires. As Moroni said in Ether 12:6, our faith was tried. Two of our investigators, who had firm baptismal dates set, canceled days before their baptisms. Although there was some initial disappointment, to our surprise we felt at peace. Deep inside we both knew our desires would be granted. We continued to put our trust in the Lord, and erased any negative or doubting thoughts that were placed into our minds.

"Shortly thereafter, while we were attending a Fast and Testimony Meeting, the answer to our prayers came. As Sister Miranda shared her testimony, she mentioned that her grandson, Robert, wanted to be baptized. We were then impressed to visit Sister Miranda and ask her about Robert. Soon after, much to our excitement, we received permission from his non-member parents to teach him the discussions.

"Meanwhile, as we were following up with one of our investigators, Joelle, she expressed to us that she wanted to put behind her all the obstacles that were preventing her from getting baptized, and just do it! Since we had been closely working with her for several months, we could hardly contain our excitement as we drove home that evening! We were honored to witness Joelle's special baptism a few days later.

"As we began teaching Robert, we were thrilled to learn that he had a younger brother and sister that were baptismal age and who wanted to participate in the discussions with him. It was quite a challenge teaching three young children, but they were eager to learn and had a great desire to be baptized. We finished up the discussions in about two weeks, and with the parent's approval, the children were baptized on June 30, the last day of the month. It was a great experience for us to help fulfill Sister Miranda's desire of bringing her family into the Gospel.

"Learning this material has opened new doors for us in accomplishing the work we were called to do. We owe a special thanks to Sister Ringger for sharing what she had discovered with us, showing us the way to increase our faith in the Lord, and achieving our righteous desires through doubting not. 'For whatsoever is born of God overcometh the world: and this is the victory that overcometh the world, even our faith. Who is he that overcometh the world, but he that believeth that Jesus is the Son of God?' –1 John 5:4-5"

Two Elders Used Their Faith

Another missionary story has to do with two Elders in

the Arizona Tempe Mission. Elder Eberhardt, and Elder Jones used their faith in a similar way as follows: First, they wrote down their Desires that people would come to them. Then they presented these Hopes to the Lord every day in their prayers and as a prayer in their thoughts all day.

1. Father, wilt thou cause a desire to come into the hearts of people in our area to ask questions about the gospel to their member neighbors.
2. Wilt thou give courage to the members to call us on the phone and ask for us to come over to teach their neighbors.
3. All things are possible unto thee, dear Father, in the name of Jesus Christ we ask of thee the Righteous Desires of our Hearts knowing that they will be according to our Faith. Even as the Brother of Jared had Faith, so have we. [I know that Jesus Christ lives and I Doubt Not]

As they daily prayed in this manner, by the third day they began to receive a call a day for ten days in a row. Members would joyously express: "Elders, you will never guess what happened to me yesterday." Then they would tell of how a neighbor came over to ask them questions about the church and desired to know more and would invite the Elders to come on over to teach them. What? By our Faith we can attract more success than we are now having? Yes!

A teenager called the Elders on the phone one morning and told of an unusual situation which happened to her the evening before. As she and a friend were walking toward the Mesa, Az. Temple, taking advantage of a nice evening, they saw a friend, with whom they had graduated from high school, sitting in front of a church reading his Bible. Just kind of jokingly they went up to him and asked, "What happened? Have you been kicked out of your church?" He looked up at them kind of surprised and said, "Well yes. The minister said that I was asking too many questions."

The LDS girls asked what his questions were and he went on to tell them that he had questions about where he would go after death and different things like that. The girls answered his questions the best that they could, then explained that: In our church we have missionaries who answer questions. This is what they do and they will not be offended no matter what question you ask." The girls called up the missionaries to set up an appointment. Their friend was baptized within three weeks even though the 'Spoiler' tried to stop his growth through Anti-Mormon materials and the negative words of friends.

The principle which we find in the city of Enoch, being of One Heart And One Mind, comes into my mind as I listened to the experiences of Elder Jones and Elder Eberhardt. These two missionaries were of One Heart and One Mind and thus they were able to ask and receive. They presented their petition to the Lord, acknowledging that they knew all things are possible unto Him. Therefore, as the missionaries asked for their Desires, the Miracle could be given because of their Faith. During the day they had no wavering Thoughts in their Minds and thus they stayed Single-Minded and thus were able to receive from the Lord.

There really is a pattern that we can follow to also receive the Righteous Desires of our Hearts.

More Miracles To Help Families

The following are true stories. However, names have been changed to protect the privacy or the individuals.

Mike and Lorrie Anne Jones of Mesa, Arizona present one striking example. Lorrie Anne felt like they were on the verge of divorce and financial ruin when she was directed to Carolyn Ringger's Faith Unpuzzled Counseling program. Through it they were able to find greater faith in God and each other, and to save a troubled marriage from disintegration. They were experiencing not only financial but spiritual troubles as well. Lorrie Anne had lost faith in Mike and, as she expressed it, had even forgotten how to pray. Their story is a long one, so I will cite just portions of it here.

When Lorrie Anne was introduced to the Faith Unpuzzled concepts and given the assignments shared in this material, her life slowly changed. For many months she struggled in an attempt to overcome her terrible negative thought and talk patterns, plus the pain due to the many problems assailing them in their marriage. When Lorrie Anne realized that what she talked about was what she was attracting to her, she began to take charge of her thoughts. She exercised her faith to "Resist the devil" and Erase all negative thoughts. She was assigned to write down her desires and pray over them and to learn to listen to the whisperings of the Spirit from the Lord.

Then the first miracle happened. She said: "I remember vividly right where I was on the road when inspiration came to me. It seemed that I heard a voice which said, 'You have not been put on this earth to approve or disapprove, only to forgive.'

"That was the beginning of the change. From that moment I started practicing, or trying to practice the truth of that insight. I had learned how to Erase negative thoughts and to think about my desires. Through this enlightenment to my mind, I came to realize that it doesn't matter what trials I had to endure, but only how I endured them. And it is that upon which we will be judged at the time of judgment."

"Then," she continued, "another miracle happened. Just 21 days before the foreclosure of our newly finished house, the state came through with the money. (They were buying the house which was in the path of a new freeway.) Mike had put his life into building and completing it, but the Spirit had said, 'Sell it. Walk away from it,' so we did.

"When we found the lovely home we live in now, the Spirit witnessed that this was right for us. We went ahead and bought it and were able to pay for it in cash from the money we received from the state. So now every day in our prayers we thank God for our new, paid-for home. We all feel that it was indeed a gift from God."

Mike tells his side of the story. He was apparently able to express more faith than Lorrie Anne for he says, "I had faith in her but I knew she didn't have faith in me. I knew we could build the first house and use it to get out of debt. Then as she started to follow the assignments given her in the counseling, I began to see where she started having a little faith in me. I began to feel that I was wanted and needed. She started showing me she cared, she had faith in me as a husband. Then I started doing more for her. As a man puts money into his home, and time and love into his marriage and family, he doesn't want a divorce. I didn't want a divorce. I didn't want to have to start all over again. I've learned to listen to my wife more now though.

"Life is still a challenge but not as bad. We didn't do it all on our own. We prayed. I prayed. I got in my car and drove down the road, praying that things would get better. Our miracle was real. We haven't missed a day to thank the Lord for what we have today."

I Found An Answer To My Prayer
The following is the story of a young woman convert and how she overcame evil thoughts by faith.

"I joined the Church when I was 19, under the most adverse circumstances. But the trials made my testimony and my commitment to the Gospel stronger. After I joined the Church I had hopes of many faith-promoting experiences. However, after I had been in the Church about six months I experienced evil thoughts coming into my mind, as you (Sister Ringger) say you had, then accusing me of being no good because I was having the wrong kind of thoughts.

"I can say I have never been through a more dark and painful time. It was rough on a 19 year-old girl who is the only member in her family. The only one I had to confide in was the Lord, because I was afraid if I spoke to someone else they wouldn't understand, and would think I was evil.

"I battled it out through fasting, prayer, and scripture study. And as the evil came, so it went. I felt like I had been through the refiner's fire. I was grateful that the Lord had delivered me. But I couldn't understand why I went through this trial.

I have now been married in the temple and we have five lovely children. Yet over the years since that time this evil has still descended upon me periodically. I have had blessings, but still I haven't had the comfort of understanding "why?" I still felt as though I was an unworthy person in the Church because of these thoughts, even though most of the time I knew I was "a good and clean person."

"This problem of evil thoughts has bothered me deeply. I just 'knew' that 'there wasn't another sister in the Gospel' who had been through this experience. For eleven years I have prayed for understanding, and have been comforted by the Holy Ghost that someday the Lord would reveal this understanding to me. I was beginning to think that it wouldn't happen until I left this life. But tonight has been an answer to a prayer for which I have been patiently waiting. Thank you so much for your talk, giving me the Light I needed."

Your Sister In Hemet, California. 1985.

Comments From Other Letters:

"My patriarchal blessing said to cultivate the quality of faith. I have for many years pondered and searched on how to accomplish this admonition. Thank you so much for sharing your Light and Knowledge with me. I have a better understanding now of how to proceed, and I will WORK on it. You have truly helped me solve my puzzle on how to make Faith become Unpuzzled and relate to my mind."
Mary White, Thatcher, Arizona, June 5, 1989

Dear Sister Carolyn:

I wish to thank you in writing, for the blessing you have been to our lives. We appreciate your sharing the principles you discovered, in the scriptures, with us. By applying these principles, we've had some positive things occur in several areas: 1) Spiritual Growth, 2) Marriage, 3) Family, and 4) Income.

First of all, our prayers are different, we think more seriously about what we pray for, and how we ask. We've found significant improvement in above-mentioned areas, and we have a renewed knowledge that "Our Heavenly Father" indeed listens, is mindful of our desires and needs, and that "He" really loves us.

As a husband and wife, we've grown closer; problems are talked out in a calmer fashion, as we know "Our Father" is a part of our team too! We are Happier.

One child, who has had some serious problems, is correcting those problems, and is growing closer to the

Lord in so doing. Our source of income has increased, which gives us hope of being free of debt in a few years, (other than our home) and we now hope to be able to fill a full-time mission when called.

Thank you. We have had these scriptures all of our lives, but you have given us the key, to open the door and use them properly. May "Our Heavenly Father" bless you for showing us these righteous principles. I'm sure He loves you for the good work you do. We know that we love you for sharing with us.

Sincerely, Betty Faye and Buddy McCain, Mesa, Az.

A Letter From Globe, Arizona – A Visit Of Peace

Like many, we set a goal to go to the Temple each month. It was two hours away which meant that it was at least a six hour trip. We had five young children and I hated to leave them. Not because they would be too sad or because I didn't trust those I left them with, but because I had a testimony that Satan was real and I was afraid of what might happen while I was gone.

In the days that followed I listened to the wrong thoughts and let fear grow strong in my heart. Each month grew to be a greater and greater struggle for me to leave my precious little ones and go to the Temple to serve the Lord. I had been praying and trying to have faith so that I could have peace.

In the late Spring we were introduced to Faith Unpuzzled. Many times that night the Spirit bore witness of the truths of these messages. We felt like we had been given new Light and Knowledge.

I felt a new sense of freedom as I realized that all the bad thoughts I had were not my own. I was free to decide which voice I would listen to and which thoughts would be mine.

I began to pray constantly for a feeling of peace concerning our trips to the Temple. All day I thought about it and tried to replace each negative thought with a good one. I listened to the tape and read the book Faith Unipuzzled often for encouragement. I also made a greater effort to read my scriptures every day. I tried in earnest to use my faith in behalf of a feeling of peace that I earnestly desired.

It was time to leave for the Temple again and it was all I could do to get myself out the door. I felt more afraid than ever before. I told my husband that I just didn't understand why it was so hard for me. I desperately didn't want to leave my children and yet I felt a real importance in going.

As the session began it was as if I couldn't keep up with my thoughts. I was learning all kinds of things; about my calling as Primary President, about my husband and children and their needs. Then I heard a voice say "Julie." I turned to find my sister, Marie, who had died as an infant when I was eight years old. I remember being surprised how much like my younger sister, Jane, she was. She was beautiful. She was standing in the aisle, her feet not touching the ground. She was smiling and I knew immediately that she loved me.

I thought "You're not dead! You're alive! You're not still a little baby buried up in Idaho! You're alive!" I was given to know that she was a Celestial Being.

We spoke to each other, but not as mortals speak. It was through our minds – our thought. She said, "It's very important for you to go to the Temple every month. And you don't have to worry anymore because I will watch over your children for you." She smiled again and was gone. And I knew where. To my house to watch over my little ones.

I was filled with joy and gratitude. I was overwhelmed with the kindness of our Father. And I was filled with peace.

After the session, in the dressing room, I was pondering what had happened when I again felt Marie's presence. She said, "Please tell Mom and Dad that I love them."

Can you imagine what a wonderful experience this was? Not only to have gained a peace toward leaving my little ones to attend the Temple, but also to have received a Heavenly visit from my sister. A sister who was not sleeping in the grave but was very much alive and ready and willing to help me! How great are the gifts of our God!

I marvel that this experience happened to me. I testify that it did on June 23, 1988 in the Arizona Temple.

I have since come upon this scripture:

7. For God hath not given us the spirit of fear; but of power, and of love, and of a sound mind.

8. Be not therefore ashamed of the testimony of our Lord, ... but be thou partakers of the afflictions of the gospel according to the power of God;

9. Who hath saved us, and called us with an holy calling, ... According to his own purpose and grace, which was given us in Christ Jesus before the world began. -- 2 Timothy 1:7-9

Julie Burk; Globe, Az.

A Missionary Discovers Faith Unpuzzled
How Elder Steven Bush Learned to Fine Tune His Missionary Work By His Faith In Christ
My name is Elder Steven Bush and I am from Farmington, Utah. I have been out in the mission field now for 18 months (July 1989) in the Arizona, Tempe mission. Sister Ringger has asked me to share

my experiences on how Faith Unpuzzled has helped me in my mission and in my life.

I came to my mission with a great zeal and conviction of the truth of the gospel and the message that I was to teach, but I was experiencing doubt, confusion and negative feelings. I was just not having the success that I knew I should have. I was trying to self-motivate and that just isn't enough. I knew why I was here, but I didn't really know how to accomplish that huge task of finding people to teach, and then of teaching them successfully.

I felt much confusion on how I could grow in faith and become single-minded so I could have more help from the Lord in finding and teaching people to baptize. I didn't understand how the Spirit speaks to us either. Answers had come into my mind in my own tone of voice, but I had not recognized that this is the way that the Lord answers our prayers.

I'd been out about four months in June 1988 when President Woolsey called another zone conference down in Tucson where I was then serving. He announced that there would be a guest speaker, Sister Carolyn Ringger, from Mesa, and she would be speaking on materials from her book, FAITH UNPUZZLED.

I was feeling down. I didn't really want to be there, and when I heard that the speaker was to be a woman I thought, "Oh great! A lady is going to talk to us.

What can a woman teach us about missionary work?" At first I didn't feel like listening. That's the male ego for you.

Then she began her talk. "We are all intelligences," she said, "and intelligences think. You talk to yourself 77% of your life and are probably having an inner mental chit-chat right now." I thought, "Yeah, I am thinking right now all right." She continued, "You may not know it, but if you are not being as successful as you would like to be, you are being double-minded."

That hit me. It was as though she was talking right to me. I wanted to jump up and say, "I am not being double-minded." But another voice deep inside said to me, "Yes, you are." It was then that I knew she was speaking truth. I decided right then that maybe I'd better pay attention and listen to what she had to say, that maybe this was the answer I had been asking for from my Heavenly Father.

I had felt before I went down to that zone conference that the Spirit was preparing me for something and would somehow answer my prayers of needing his help. As Sister Ringger continued her talk the Spirit touched my heart and I began to understand how my desire to grow closer to my Heavenly Father could be fulfilled. She explained about our inner self-talk and how to program our subconscious mind so as to erase negative thoughts and replace them with positive thoughts. She spoke of praying for Light and Knowledge to help us find answers and make right decisions, and then of opening up our inner heart and mind to listen to the Lord's promptings. She talked about how to grow in faith and become more single-minded to the Lord in all our missionary work and in our lives.

These were the answers I needed and I decided I would begin immediately to put them into practice. I wrote up a list of desires which I wanted to accomplish and began reciting them to myself each night as I went to bed, etching it upon my brain cells, that my brain-servant would know how I wanted it to work for me. I was fine tuning my spirit to be in tune with the Spirit of the Lord and the Holy Ghost so that I could hear the Still Small Voice. After I had said my prayers, I would go over and over in my mind the ten basic goals I had set for myself, beginning with the foundation goal of gaining greater faith in the Lord Jesus Christ. I sincerely repeated over and over to myself these great soul filling truths: 1)"I love Jesus Christ, 2) I know that Jesus Christ lives, 3) I doubt not that He lives, 4) I would do anything for Jesus Christ." I took the ideas she taught and allowed the Spirit to make them individual for me. The instructions came into my mind as positive thoughts, and I used them in my own way.

As I adapted the truths to an Elder Bush version, I saw in my mind's eye, a kind of computer wheel or disk. On the disk I saw imprinted only positive thoughts, and as it went around and around, I continued to focus it on single-minded, positive thoughts and fed those thoughts into the computer of my mind until good thoughts completely filled it. There was no room then for the negative and so they would just bounce off. Sometimes though, when they did affect me I would have to dismiss them in the name of Jesus Christ, and they would leave. There was a time for awhile when I started having doubts and I allowed my computer disk to start spinning backwards. It took a lot of work and faith to set my thoughts right and get it spinning in the right direction again.

I was impressed by the Spirit to start asking for: "Light and Knowledge" on how Faith works, and when I did, the Spirit led me to Alma 17:2-4. Alma and the sons of Mosiah met again after serving on missions for fourteen years. The brothers told Alma what they did to be successful.

2. ...therefore Alma did rejoice exceedingly to see his brethren; and what added more to his joy, they were still his brethren in the Lord; yea, and they had waxed strong in the knowledge of the truth; for they were men of a sound understanding and they had searched the scriptures diligently, that they might know the word of God.

3. But this is not all; they had given themselves to much prayer, and fasting; therefore they had the spirit of prophecy, and the spirit of revelation, and when

they taught, they taught with power and authority of God

4. And they had been teaching the word of God for the space of fourteen years among the Lamanites, having had much success in bringing many to the knowledge of the truth; yea, by the power of their words many were brought before the altar of God, to call on his name and confess their sins before him.
-- Alma 17:2-4

After being directed to Alma 17, I started to think to myself, "If they could do it, I could do it!" I have applied this in all of my missionary efforts and I have had great success because of it.

When I knock on people's doors they will let my companion and me in because I know what I am here for. I know that Jesus Christ is behind us in this work and will help us teach His word so that the people will recognize its truth and power.

I prayed for Light and Knowledge about everything that we did. I asked Him to lead us to the homes of those who would be willing to listen and to hear about the Lord Jesus Christ. And I asked Him to guide me in the words I should say to them, and to prepare the minds of the people so they would be ready to receive our message. I sought always to be open to the promptings of the Spirit.

I taught these truths to my companions and they also had great success which brought me great joy. We made a commitment to the Lord that we would seek always to have His Spirit in our heart, never doubting. We asked for His guidance in all that we did. While in Tucson, we asked in great faith for the TV media referrals to be sent to us to teach the families who sent them. We said that we would go to each family and teach them as His representatives. Soon referrals started to arrive to us, sixty in all. The other missionaries asked me why they didn't receive any. Then I realized what we had done. We had asked for the referrals. We asked and doubted not and it came to pass. We hoped for something that we didn't see. As Mormon 9:21 describes the experience, so it began to happen to us.

21. Behold, I say unto you that whoso believeth in Christ, doubting nothing, whatsoever he shall ask the Father in the name of Christ it shall be granted him; and this promise is unto all, even unto the ends of the earth.

We took the referrals we received seriously and prayed over each one of them. We placed their names by our bedside at night before we went to bed and asked for the Light and Knowledge we would need to help them. In the morning I would know what we needed to do for them. What a thrill to be a tool in the Lord's hand. We kept a prayer in our heart (thoughts) all day plus at their door step we again would request for the Light and Knowledge we needed to say exactly what the referral family needed. The ideas were given us into our minds. Things each family needed. D&C 100:5 describes this experience:

5. Therefore, verily I say unto you; lift up your voices unto this people; speak the thoughts that I shall put into your hearts, and you shall not be confounded before men;

It may appear repetitious that I should keep stressing how important it is to keep asking for Light and Knowledge always, in every situation, but it works! Our Heavenly Father directed us, and we were successful. And of those 60 referrals which we had received that month, twenty of them were baptized!

Elder Hook, my new companion who came to me in November also had a great missionary spirit of faith, never doubting. I taught him these principles too and we prayed for Light and Knowledge over all of our contacts. That one month we had 73 discussions with investigators for just one ward and ten baptisms.

I would like to tell about another experience we had while I was there in Tucson. I had been made District Leader and we had a couple of companionships who had some "eternal investigators." These people were doing all the right things. They were studying the book of Mormon, but they still hadn't committed to be baptized. The missionaries didn't know quite what was wrong. So I called a District Meeting to discuss the situation, and ask for ideas on what we could do to help these people to take that necessary step of baptism. The Elders and Sisters listed many great ideas but we had tried all of these things and they just hadn't worked.

Then the thought came into my mind that we needed to invite these people to witness a baptism. I challenged the Elders and Sisters to bring their investigators with them to our next baptism; and as I did we could feel the Spirit of the Lord present, confirming that this was the step which we should take.

My companion and I had a baptism scheduled for four of our investigators on the following Sunday. The Sisters and the Elders each brought a family of four to that baptism, for a total of eight investigators present. During the baptismal service we again felt the spirit of the Lord present, and the investigators must have felt it too because after the service every one of them came up to me, and requested to be baptized that night. They didn't want to wait until the next week even. However, since it was 9 p.m., we scheduled their baptismal service for the next day, Monday. And every one of those eight people were baptized at that time! That experience was a real testimony to me of the guidance and promptings of the Spirit.

Then in December something happened. I allowed Satan to creep in with his doubting thoughts. I began to think to myself, "Does this really work?" I decided I wanted to experiment. So I thought, "I'll just pray for understanding instead of Light and Knowledge, to see if the things I am doing are really right." Of course that was a doubt. I began to be double-minded again like at the beginning of my mission. My attitude changed. Everybody noticed it, not only the Elders, Sisters and members, but even the investigators we were working with noticed it. One side affect was that we stopped getting referrals.

December was a terrible month. I had allowed doubt back into my life and all of our work was affected. The thoughts I fought were real and they came into my mind in my own tone of voice fooling me totally. This was the month we could call home and I did not have that great missionary spirit of optimism like the months before. Where had it gone to? I had allowed the Spoiler's doubt to enter my mind unaware. (Be on guard people. Do not think about negative truths, they are still negative. Fine tune your thoughts, request Light and Knowledge and you will be guided. Even ask for angels to be with you to go before you to prepare the minds of people you will meet, and it will be so.)

January came and I was still feeling depressed. This was supposed to be a time of renewal and of new beginnings. Then I was transferred to Globe as District Leader. I was in Mesa on a transfer day getting a free haircut at Martha Johnson's, when I ran into Sister Ringger again. She asked me how I was doing and if the Faith Unpuzzled concepts had helped me in my missionary work. I told her yes, that they work fine when I use them.

That encounter set me thinking and motivated me to turn myself around, and set me back on the right path again. I again committed myself to the Lord and started applying the principles of faith and prayer, asking for Light and Knowledge over all our contacts.

We were out tracting one day and met a family of eight, Jehovah Witnesses. I asked for Light and Knowledge as to what I could say to them to touch their understanding. I was given what they needed to awaken them. I could feel the spirit of the Lord there that day and we were able to teach them the Gospel and in fact, it was not too long after that they asked us if they could be baptized. The whole family of eight entered the waters of baptism, thus becoming members of The Church of Jesus Christ of Latter-day Saints.

Many people have asked me from time to time how I have been able to teach and baptize so many people. It's because I am not a doubter of Jesus Christ. I know that He lives, and that through His power all things are possible. I am human like everybody else, and I feel that anyone can do this, just as the prophets did. The KEY is our Doubting Not Faith that Jesus Christ is the son of God and that through Him all things are possible. Then by asking for Light and Knowledge; positive, pure and enlightening thoughts will come as instructions into the mind, in your own tone of voice [because it comes into your instrument of the Spirit]. We must learn to hear the Still Small Voice [arriving within each of us].

Again, read Mormon 9:18-28 as you ask for Light and Knowledge. Verse 20 tells us that it is our unbelief which stops us from having a miracle. We need to ask in the right way he says. We need to know the God in whom we should trust. What is that? "Behold, I say unto you that whoso believeth in Christ, doubting nothing [about Christ], whatsoever he shall ask the Father in the name of Christ it shall be granted him; and this promise is unto all, even unto the ends of the earth." I can now see that I am following a key scripture. Again I say, I know that Jesus Christ lives and I doubt Him not.

My challenge to you, Elders and Sisters, is to put this to a test and to apply these skills which Sister Ringger has brought forth through the Light and Knowledge given her of Heavenly Father. They take mental effort to apply which is how the law of faith works, by your mental effort. This is something which has been brought forth to help us find greater success, and to help us become pure in heart in preparation for Heavenly Father's kingdom. – Elder Steven Bush

Puzzle Piece #7
Faith Joy Cycle

Carolyn P. Ringger

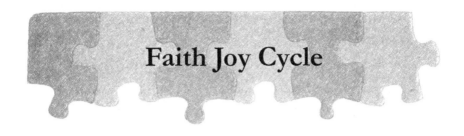

Faith Joy Cycle

The Faith – Joy Cycle

It Begins With Your Thoughts

We have now arrived at the FAITH-JOY CYCLE, how each of us may experience and discover joy. Nephi tells us in 2 Nephi 2:25 that "Men are that they might have joy." That means then that we were sent here to learn to find joy! We were sent here to learn what the steps are that will help us find joy! And then to live to experience that joy!

The theme of our book has been FAITH UNPUZZLED, with faith as the first key element in this Faith-Joy Cycle. And our lesson material has been built around how to grow in faith, that you may experience the miracle, and find joy in your life.

Enjoy the upcoming chart which shows this Faith-Joy Cycle. Notice how it always starts with your thoughts at the beginning of the cycle. Then if the cycle is followed through faithfully, you end up with a feeling of joy. As you repeat the cycle, it builds and strengthens the cycle each time and builds and strengthens your faith and joy.

Just below the Faith-Joy Cycle you will see another cycle, the Depression Cycle. Note that the beginning of this cycle also starts with your thoughts.

- Think positive thoughts about your hopes and goals- build faith and have a miracle, find joy.
- Think negative thoughts about your problems – experience depression, despair.
- Thoughts create emotions, which create your actions.

Are you wondering what P.L.O.M. in the Depression Cycle stands for? It stands for 'Poor Little Old Me.' Sound familiar?

Ok. Now let's look at the next page and spend some time studying these cycles and what their implications might be in your life.

Faith
-- Joy Cycle --

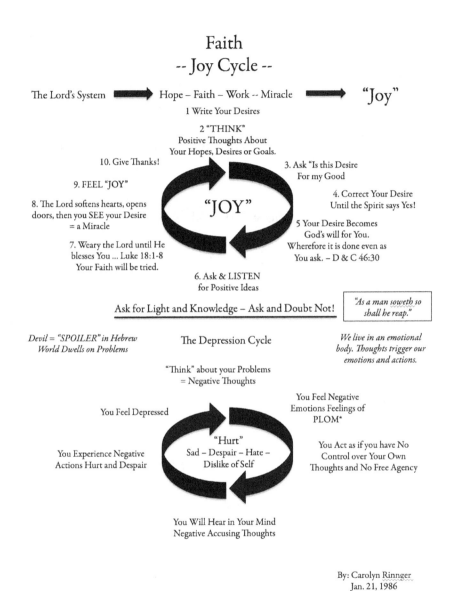

The Lord's System ➡ Hope – Faith – Work -- Miracle ➡ "Joy"

1 Write Your Desires

2 "THINK"
Positive Thoughts About
Your Hopes, Desires or Goals.

10. Give Thanks!

9. FEEL "JOY"

8. The Lord softens hearts, opens
doors, then you SEE your Desire
= a Miracle

"JOY"

3. Ask "Is this Desire
For my Good

4. Correct Your Desire
Until the Spirit says Yes!

7. Weary the Lord until He
blesses You ... Luke 18:1-8
Your Faith will be tried.

5 Your Desire Becomes
God's will for You.
Wherefore it is done even as
You ask. – D & C 46:30

6. Ask & LISTEN
for Positive Ideas

Ask for Light and Knowledge – Ask and Doubt Not!

*"As a man soweth so
shall he reap."*

*Devil = "SPOILER" in Hebrew
World Dwells on Problems*

The Depression Cycle

*We live in an emotional
body. Thoughts trigger our
emotions and actions.*

"Think" about your Problems
= Negative Thoughts

You Feel Depressed

You Feel Negative
Emotions Feelings of
PLOM*

"Hurt"
Sad – Despair – Hate –
Dislike of Self

You Experience Negative
Actions Hurt and Despair

You Act as if you have No
Control over Your Own
Thoughts and No Free Agency

You Will Hear in Your Mind
Negative Accusing Thoughts

By: Carolyn Rinnger
Jan. 21, 1986

Faith Is The First Basic Ingredient In The Faith – Joy Cycle

When you see the word Faith, remember that it has great meaning behind it. Allow a mental window of understanding to open to your inner view, like a computer can do. The computer opens up a window to show you what one word, as a command, can do for you. You can see within your mind the real meaning as it shows all of the formula, not just the word – FAITH – in hopes you might understand. Here is what you might etch on your memory cells for the word FAITH:

Each time you read the word FAITH, realize that it really means:
    1. I know Jesus Christ Lives!
    2. I Doubt Not that He lives!
    3. Whatever I ask for, which is confirmed by the Spirit of truth, is God's will for me and is coming to pass. –Mormon 9:21 --D&C 46:7, 30 --Mark 9:23-24

Also Realize Moroni 7:25-27 Reveals To Us That By Faith in Christ:
    1. You may be saved and...
    2. You may Lay Hold on every good thing.

Taking The Shield Of Faith

    17. Taking the shield of faith wherewith ye shall be able to quench all the fiery darts of the wicked.
    -- D&C 27:17

Here the Lord offers us a Shield of Faith which we may use in our struggle against the adversary. He also speaks in this same passage, of putting on the whole armor of God.

Let us examine more closely how you and I can put on this armor and take the shield of faith. The following is information we have been discussing throughout this material. We will recap and offer it now for review.

Taking The Shield Of Faith – That Ye May Find Joy

The Lord, in D&C 27:17 refers to the Shield of Faith. He also speaks of putting on the whole armor of God. He says that you must lift up your hearts and rejoice and take upon you His whole armor, having your loins girt about with truth, having on the breastplate of righteousness and your feet shod with the preparation of the gospel, taking the shield of faith wherewith ye shall be able to quench all the fiery darts, evil thoughts, of the wicked; And take the helmet of salvation, and the sword of my Spirit. (D&C 27:15-18)

The Lord is offering here a whole armor, protected ultimately with the shield of faith. And as we take on this strong defense we can lift up our hearts and rejoice. Each of us have discovered the cycle of faith to Joy.

Let us here recap this Faith-Joy Cycle as it builds in ever-growing and ever-widening circles as you repeat it over and over. This is the plan the Lord would have me use building my faith and solving my daily challenges. As we discover what the Law of Faith is, then our earth test has more experiences of joy, for the way we solve all of our problems is by faith. The quote: "By Faith all things possible", becomes a living reality.

How To Solve Your Problems By Using The Law Of Faith

1. Think about your problem or Challenge, name it.

2. Think about how you desire to solve it. Here is where you begin to formulate a plan or plans, which you will then take to the Lord. (See Ether 2:23-25 and 3:4) Request for Light and Knowledge to receive new ideas or more understanding.

3. Ask "is this desire for my good?" Ponder over the ideas then choose one. Next present it to the Lord for confirmation. If it be right then you will feel a burning or hear an inner voice speak to you. This is described in D&C 8:2-4:

Yea, behold, I will tell you in your mind and in your heart, by the Holy Ghost, which shall come upon you and which shall dwell in your heart (thoughts) --D&C 8:2

The Lord explains this process further in D&C 88:66:

66. Behold, that which you hear is as the voice of one crying in the wilderness – in the wilderness, because you cannot see him – my voice, because my voice is Spirit; my Spirit is truth. -- D&C 88:66

I believe that the wilderness spoken of here is the wilderness of our minds, with thoughts sent to us from of God, which we hear distantly in our minds, and most often in our own tone of voice. These thoughts are there, quietly trying to attract our attention. The Lord desires to help us if we will but tune our mind and heart to the voice of the Spirit.

4. When the Spirit says yes, (correct your request until you receive a yes). Do what the Spirit instructs. The ideas will be positive, pure and

enlightening. Do what you are impressed to do. This takes work. Act upon the ideas. Faith without works is dead! Or in other words, faith with works is alive and full of results, the requested miracle.

The Spirit can talk to you or give you a feeling of peace or a tingling throughout your body, which confirms your request. Once you have received this confirmation and know that it is right, you must do all you can toward its accomplishment.

5. Your Desire becomes God's will for you by asking in the Spirit. "Wherefore it is done even as he asketh." -- D&C 46:30

6. Ask and Doubt Not. I know that Christ lives, and I mentally Doubt Him Not. Therefore that which I desire in righteousness shall be granted. The Lord has promised:

21. Behold I say unto you that whoso believeth in Christ, doubting nothing, whatsoever he shall ask the Father in the name of Christ, it shall be granted him; and this promise is unto all, even unto the ends of the earth. -- Mormon 9:21

When Alma and his followers were being persecuted by Amulon because of their faith, the Lord comforted them and promised their deliverance. (See Mosiah 24:10-20). Then later, when Alma's son, Alma, and the sons of Mosiah were persecuting the saints, an angel appeared and Alma was struck dumb, and he and the sons of Mosiah were converted.

And this was due to the faith and prayers of their fathers on their behalf. (See Mosiah 27:14-22).

7. Weary the Lord until you receive your confirmed desire. Read Luke 18:1-8, which is the parable of the unjust judge. The widow, by her continuous importuning was granted her desire. Also note that the Lord expects us to take the initiative to do much good of our own free will to bring to pass much righteousness. (See D&C 58:26-27). And in D&C 9:8 he tells us to "study it out in your mind, then ye must ask me if it be right, and if it is right I will cause that your bosom will burn within you; therefore, you shall feel that it is right." (D&C 9:8)

   Remember that your faith will be tried. Ether 12:6 tells us, "wherefore dispute not because ye see not, for ye receive no witness until after the trial of your faith." Fear is one of the Spoiler's greatest weapons, fear and mistrust. And he will seek to use it to try your faith. In D&C 67:1-3, the elders were told, "There were fears in your hearts, and verily this is the reason that ye did not receive." Others the evil one will "flatter away in carnal security" telling them he is no devil and there is no hell. He simply whispers into the spiritual ear and you hear him in your mind as thoughts, in your own tone of voice often. See 2 Nephi 28:22.

8. Receive the Miracle. When you see the righteous desires of your heart being granted, you KNOW

that it is a miracle, and that it was granted unto you because of your faith. There are many recorded instances of this in the scriptures. The story of the 2,000 stripling young warriors of Helaman is an outstanding example, where they fought, and many around them were killed, both Nephites and Lamanites, but not a single one of them was killed. "...they had been taught by their mothers, that if they did not doubt God, then God would deliver them." (Alma 56:47)

And miraculously, "...there was not one soul of them who did perish; yea, and neither was there one soul among them who had not received many wounds . . . and we do justly ascribe it to the miraculous power of God, because of their exceeding faith." (Alma 57:25-26) We today have also been given miraculous promises, both personally and as a people.

One of the greatest of these is recorded in Ether 4:7, 11-12:

7. And in that day that they shall exercise faith in me, saith the Lord, even as the brother of Jared did, that they may become sanctified in me, then will I manifest unto them the things which the brother of Jared saw, even to the unfolding unto them all my revelations, saith Jesus Christ...

11. But he that believeth these things which I have spoken, him will I visit with the manifestations of my

Spirit, and he shall know and bear record . . .

12. And whatsoever persuadeth men to do good is of me; for good cometh of none save it be of me.
--Ether 4: 7, 11-12

9. FEEL JOY! (Joy is not #1 on the list. You progress toward JOY by your faith!)
10. Give Thanks! It was Nephi who said, "Men are that they might have joy." (2 Nephi 2:25) Life is not fair and it is not easy. The Spirit spoke to me and said "Life takes effort." That effort is to use Doubting Not Faith. And now that we realize this, it is time to utilize the laws of faith, and create the Joy I think Nephi was explaining. This Joy comes from learning how to solve the problems of earth life through Faith In The Lord Jesus Christ. He is the being who brings forth the miracle. We are the ones who must ask – using our faith. We connect our desires to His power.

We Are Not Human Beings Having Spiritual Experiences;

We Are Spiritual Beings Having Emotional, Human Experiences.

Earth Life Is Our School, And The Challenges We Face Are Our Homework.

This life is a great screening process. The Spirit of Light and Truth is seeking those who will be found Pure In Heart after being tested in all things. To those who pass this test will be given all that they have.

We can cleanse ourselves of our double-mindedness. Through our thoughts we can gain control and become master of ourselves. And through watching our thoughts, each of us can be found pure in heart. Our reward is that as we do this, we shall also grow and find greater joy.

Our basic nature is not evil, though the thoughts from the Spoiler would try to convince us otherwise. We are Children of God our Father, a Pure-in-Heart Being.

The Psalmist declared that "In thy presence is fullness of joy." (Psalms 16:11) and Galatians speaks of the joy we may experience here, "but the fruit of the Spirit is love, joy, peace, longsuffering, gentleness, goodness, faith." (Gal. 5:22) The Doctrine and Covenants gives us the clearest picture of what man is and how we may attain joy.

33. For man is Spirit. The elements are eternal, and spirit and element, inseparably connected, receive a fullness of joy

35. ...Yea, man is the tabernacle of God, even temples; and whatsoever temple is defiled, God shall destroy that temple.

36. The glory of god is intelligence, or, in other

words, light and truth.

37. Light and truth forsake that evil one.
--D&C 93:33-37

Now is the time to Awaken The Sleeping Giant within each of us, through the Laws of Faith. Now is the time to hold up the Shield of Faith, which shall help us find eternal joy. Remember:

MEN ARE
THAT THEY MIGHT
HAVE JOY.

MEN AND WOMEN ARE
THAT THEY MIGHT
HAVE JOY!

What Will Ye That I Should Do?

23. And the Lord said unto the brother of Jared; What will ye that I should do that ye may have light in your vessels? -- Ether 2:23

25. ... Therefore what will ye that I should prepare for you that ye may have light when ye are swallowed up in the depths of the sea? -- Ether 2:25

The Brother of Jared worked out a plan which was confirmed. How marvelous. This really is the Lords way of working with us. The Lord ask's, "what will ye that I should do [for you]?" We may follow the example of those who came before us, that used the laws of faith, and were able to achieve progress and success in this life.

Assignment
Read the whole story of the brother of Jared, in the book of Mormon: Ether Chapters: 1 – 15.

Puzzle Piece #8
Zion Is Pure In Heart

Carolyn P. Ringger

Zion Is The Pure In Heart

The Millennium Is Zion . . .

Zion Is . . .
The Pure In Heart.
> Therefore, verily, thus saith the Lord, Let Zion rejoice,
> for this is Zion – THE PURE IN HEART; therefore,
> let Zion rejoice, while all the wicked shall mourn.
> --D&C 97:21

The Pure In Heart Shall Inherit Zion
> 17. Zion shall not be moved out of her place,
> notwithstanding her children are scattered. They that
> remain, and are pure in heart, shall return and come to
> their inheritances, they and their children, with songs
> of everlasting joy, to build up the waste places of Zion.
> --D&C 101:17-18

How Can We Use This Material To Prepare For The
Millennium?

Our Best Defense:

"We do not say that all of the saints will be spared and saved from the coming day of desolation. But we do say there is no promise of safety and no promise of security except for those who love the Lord and who are seeking to do all that he commands."
--Bruce R. McConkie, Ensign, May 1979, p. 93

And Satan Shall Be Bound

I have spent many hours pondering over the events which have been prophesied yet to come. Uppermost in my mind is the Second coming and Millennial reign of Christ upon the earth. Here are some scriptures concerning this era of time:

1. And I saw an angel come down from heaven, having the key of the bottomless pit and a great chain in his hand.

2. And he laid hold on the dragon, that old serpent, which is the Devil, and Satan, and bound him a thousand years. --Revelation 20:1-2

26. And because of the righteousness of his people, Satan has no power; wherefore, he cannot be loosed for the space of many years; for he hath *no power over the hearts (thoughts and feelings)* of the people, for they dwell in righteousness, and the Holy One of Israel reigneth. --1 Nephi 22:26

55. And Satan shall be bound, that he shall have *no*

place in the hearts of the children of men, ...
-- D&C 45:55

31. For Satan shall be bound, and when he is loosed again he shall only reign for a little season, and then cometh the end of the earth.

32. And he that liveth in righteousness shall be changed in the twinkling of an eye, and earth shall pass away so as by fire. --D&C 43:31-32

50. And he that liveth when the Lord shall come, and hath kept the faith, blessed is he; nevertheless, it is appointed to him to die at the age of man.

51. Wherefore, children shall grow up until they become old; old men shall die; but they shall not sleep in the dust, but they shall be changed in the twinkling of an eye. --D&C 63:50-51

29. And there shall be no sorrow because there is no death.

30. In that day an infant shall not die until he is old; and his life shall be as the age of a tree;

31. And when he dies he shall not sleep, that is to say in the earth, but shall be changed in the twinkling of an eye, and shall be caught up, and his rest shall be glorious. --D&C 101:29-31

During the Millennial reign, we know that Satan will have no evil influence upon the (thoughts and feeling) hearts of the children of men. All people shall live to the age of a tree, no early deaths, and then they shall be changed from mortality to immortality in the twinkling of an eye, or accorder to Ringger 2:2 "Twinkled!"

What magnificent promises the Millennium holds for us! It will be a time of peace and joy. Our leaders have been preparing us with the realization that we are in that era of time – we and our seed will be the people who will live to usher in that event. This being true, it must also be true that we are the generation who must learn to bind Satan, for it will not be done with chains, but because we listen to him no more. (From The Millennial Messiah, McConkie, p. 666-669)

As you can see by the study of this material, we can make this great binding of evil occur. How many Awakened People will it take, people who really are working daily to be more pure in heart, to become like the City of Zion?

When we have learned how to watch over our thoughts, then we as parents are the ones who must teach our children so that they will have the Faith like unto the Sons of Helaman. We must be trustworthy as were the mothers of the 2,000 young men, for they doubted not that their Mothers knew that God lives and would care for them, upon their prayer of Faith. We are the Fathers and Mothers who can overcome the wickedness of our time. This Earth life is not our beginning, the Earth time is our test to see if we will choose Good over Evil. The daily challenges are real but these challenges are our homework!

We are "Live Receiving Sets" attuned to spiritual communications which we cannot see. We can tune in to the positive station which gives off Light and Knowledge. We must "Ask, and it shall be given you; seek, and ye shall find; knock, and it shall be opened unto you:" (Matthew 7:7). We need to ask for information in order to open up the Positive airways, whereas, the opposite station from the Spoiler needs no invitation at all. It is always blaring to our spirits. We pick up the thoughts, wrestle with them, and accept or reject them one by one. This takes from us a great deal of energy in these mental battles.

We have shown you in this material that you only need to exert your mental effort to stop this tapping of your mental energy, through the simple technique of Mentally Saying, "I delete and erase that thought." This quickly cancels any reception of the flow of negative thoughts which always seek a way in for those who allow it and who feel they have no control over their thoughts. Proverbs describe it well: "He that hath no rule over his own spirit [thoughts] is like a city that is broken down, and without walls." (Proverbs 25:28)

Remember, if any negative thoughts come into your mind, such as:
1. Being unforgiving of someone.
2. Belittling yourself or someone else.
3. Comparing of self in a negative way.
4. Criticizing yourself.
5. Feelings of "I can't"
6. Degrading or filthy words.
7. Feelings of anger.
8. Desire to see R, NC17 or any unclean movie or magazine or pornography
9. Desire to smoke, use liquor or drugs, etc.

Simply say, "Delete" or "I Scramble That Thought," and your energy will cut it off! You are in control. By your Faith in the Lord Jesus Christ, you gain that control. You are connecting your energy and desires with His Power and He can do ALL things. Then ask for light and knowledge & replace all negative positive thoughts with positive thoughts.

If great numbers of Christian People will apply this knowledge, I can see where we will finally be doing something on our part in fulfilling the scripture, "And Satan shall be bound that he shall have no place in the hearts of the children of men." (D&C 45:55) They will realize how evil input occurs and they will be able to shut off the signal, for they have Cancelled their reception of it.

We are not to be commanded in all things. It is time for us to use our own agency in a way which will have a great effect upon mankind. We can help change the history of our generation by catching a concept which I learned from the comment of a friend. Here is the story:

In the book entitled, *The Hundredth Monkey,* by Tim Keyes, is recorded a pattern of behavior by a certain group of monkeys on the Japanese island of Koshima. These monkeys ate sweet potatoes dropped there by the scientists as part of their diet. The older monkeys never washed their food before eating it. Then the researchers noticed one younger monkey which began one day to rinse off the sweet potato before eating it. Next they noticed a few other monkeys copying the first monkey by washing their food also. Apparently they liked the results. You can appreciate that the food would be less gritty with no dirt or sand on it. It took six years for the idea of washing their food to really catch on. Then the researchers noticed that suddenly, as if overnight all of the monkeys on the island knew how to wash their food before eating it. Through the idea used by one creative monkey, all of the other monkeys were able to follow the new pattern. Then, as if the knowledge jumped – all of the monkeys on the small island began to wash their potatoes

As I pondered the above idea which a friend had presented, it came to me that there is a saturation point where one person can make a difference to a whole society. Slowly at first, as the truths we have discussed here begin to take hold, individuals, then family members, friends, and all Christians can cause the effect of these truths to widen and grow until all who so desire can know and improve their lives. These ideas of how to apply the law of **Faith** and **How We Can Become Pure In Heart Are Real And Do-Able!** Over the last twenty years, filth has increased and flooded our land. Now is the time for us to cause **Faith To Flood The Land** through the righteous desires of people who are pure in **Heart.**

We started out with the following chart on page 5, to show that your positive inner thoughts about your desires and your testimony of the Savior really do matter. We can match up with each of the three steps. Read the chart again now that many, many truths have been shared.

Faith = You Believe In Jesus Christ = Your Positive Inner
Self-Talk About Christ =
You Doubt Not that He Lives and That He Can Do All
Things = You Are SINGLE-MINDED

Jesus Christ Lives. When you know that Jesus Christ Lives and you DOUBT HIM NOT, you have Faith in Him!

Read Mormon 9:18-27.

He is Pure In Heart. When you repent and are watching over your thoughts, you become Pure in Heart, your inner vessel is cleansed and you can receive what you ask for. Read Mosiah 4:30, 1 John 3:2-3.

He Can Do All Things. You can hook up your Hopes and Desires with HIS POWER by being Single Minded. You then have FAITH. Miracles are real today by Faith in Jesus Christ. Read Moroni 7:20-30 and Mosiah 24:10-17.

You Can Become Of One Mind And One Heart With The Lord, or Pure in All of Your Thoughts.

If not this technique, WHAT? If not us, WHO? If not now, WHEN? It is the time for all good people to exert personal daily effort to make this world better. WE CAN DO IT!! Realize that...

Zion Is The "Pure" In "Heart"

The Pure In "Heart" Shall See God – Matt 5:8

How Will Satan Be Bound During The Millennium?

According to D&C 43:31 Satan shall be bound (during the Millennium) then loosed for a little season, and then will come the end. How will this come about? The Doctrine and Covenants Student Manual for Religion, 1985-86, p. 89

explains this as follows:

> Nephi, in speaking of the Millennial Era, said that "because of the righteousness of his [the Lord's] people, Satan has no power; wherefore, he cannot be loosed for the space of many years; for he hath no power over the hearts of the people, for they dwell in righteousness, and the Holy One of Israel reigneth.
> --1 Nephi 22:26

President Joseph Fielding Smith taught about the binding of Satan:

> "There are many among us who teach that the binding of Satan will be merely the binding which those dwelling on the earth will place upon him by their refusal to hear his enticing. This is not so. He will not have the privilege during that period of time to tempt any man. (D&C 101:28)" (Church History and Modern Revelation, 1;192.)

These two statements at first may seem to be at variance, but in reality they are not. It is true that Satan cannot exert power over them. The restrictions that will come upon Satan will be a result of two important actions by the Lord: (1) He will destroy Telestial wickedness from the earth at his second coming; and (2) As a reward for those who heed his counsels, the Lord will pour out His Spirit upon the righteous who remain to the extent that Satan's power will be overwhelmed. Thus, Satan will not have power to tempt or negatively influence the Lord's people. Both the righteousness of the Saints and operation of the Lord's power are necessary to bind Satan. If the Saints do not give heed to God's word, he will not impart of His Spirit; and if the Lord's influence is not brought to bear to aid the Saints, they on their own power, cannot withstand the force of the adversary.

President George Q. Cannon explained how both the power of God and the righteousness of the Saints are necessary to bind Satan:

> "We talk about Satan being bound. Satan will be bound by the power of God; but he will be bound also by the determination of the people of God not to listen to him, not to be governed by him. The Lord will not bind him and take his power from the earth while there are men and women willing to be governed by him. That is contrary to the plan of salvation. To deprive men of their agency is contrary to the purposes of our God." [See 2 Nephi 2:11. To preserve agency it is necessary to be enticed by opposing forces.]

And Finally, Scriptures Tell Their Own Story

We have been using many scriptures. Now let us do an uncommon thing by placing these scriptures together like puzzle pieces and see how they flow. The scriptures tell their own story.

FAITH

> 20. And now, my brethren, how is it possible that ye can lay hold upon every good thing?

> 21. And now I come to that faith, of which I said I would speak; and I will tell you the way whereby ye may lay hold on every good thing. -- Moroni 7:20-21

HOPE

40. And again, my beloved brethren, I would speak unto you concerning hope. How is it that ye can attain unto faith, save ye shall have hope? --Moroni 7:40

FAITH-HOPE

1. Now faith is the substance of things hoped for, the evidence of things not seen.

(JST Now faith is the assurance of things hoped for, the proof of things not seen.) -- Hebrews 11:1

ASK, SEEK KNOCK

5. If any of you lack wisdom, let him ask of God, that giveth to all men liberally, and upbraideth not; and it shall be given him,

6. But let him ask in faith, nothing wavering. For he that wavereth is like a wave of the sea driven with the wind and tossed.

7. For let not that man think that he shall receive anything of the Lord.

8. A double minded man is unstable in all his ways

--James 1:5-8
NOTHING WAVERING

3. Ye ask, and receive not, because ye ask amiss...

7. Submit yourselves therefore to God. Resist the devil, and he will flee from you.

8. Draw nigh to God, and he will draw nigh to you. Cleanse your hands, ye sinners; and purify your hearts, ye double minded. -- James 4:3, 7-8

LISTEN- SPIRITUAL COMMUNICATION

2. I will tell you in your mind and in your heart, by the Holy Ghost, which shall come upon you and which shall dwell in your heart.

3. Now, behold, this is the spirit of revelation; behold, this is the spirit by which Moses brought the children of Israel through the Red Sea on dry ground.

4. Therefore this is thy gift; apply unto it, and blessed art thou... –D&C 8:2-4, 8-10

THE MIRACLE COMES THROUGH CHRIST

25. Men began to exercise faith in Christ; and thus by faith, they did lay hold upon every good thing; and thus it was until the coming of Christ.

26. And after that he came <u>men also were saved by faith in his name;</u> and as surely as Christ liveth he spake these words unto our fathers, saying: <u>Whatsoever thing ye shall ask the Father in my name, which is good, in faith believing that ye shall receive, behold, it shall be done unto you.</u> -- Moroni 7:25-26

BELIEVE IN CHRIST

21. <u>Whoso believeth in Christ, doubting nothing, whatsoever he shall ask the Father in the name of Christ it shall be granted him;</u> and this promise is unto all, --Mormon 9:32

Now go back three pages and read only the underlined portions of the scriptures and listen as the scriptures tell their own story.

Two of Our Most Important Goals On Earth Are:

1. To Become Pure In Heart By Watching Over Our Thoughts! (Mosiah 4:30)

2. And Learn How The Law of Faith Works and By Our Faith In Jesus Christ, Doubting Not, We Can Fulfill All Things and Solve All Problems. (Mormon 9:21 & Moroni 7:25-26)

Puzzle Piece #9
You + Your Testimony

You + Your Testimony

You + Your Testimony of JESUS CHRIST, Make Up The Final PUZZLE PIECE!

This Piece Makes It Possible, For You To Make All, Of The Other Pieces Fit!

You Are A Very Important Person In Your Life

You are one of the most important people you will ever know because only you can develop your own testimony in Jesus Christ. Only you can think the thoughts you have. Only you can learn to "Erase" all negative thoughts from your mind then ask for Light and Knowledge from the Lord. Only you can get you to follow the Lord Jesus Christ and become Pure in your own heart, your thoughts.

"You Are One of The MOST Important People YOU Will Ever Know."
Only You Think Your Thoughts and Only YOU Can Get YOU To Follow Jesus Christ." -

- Carolyn Ringger

221

We Are Begotten Sons And Daughters Unto God

6. Ye are gods; and all of you are children of the most high. -- Psalms 82:6

10. Ye are the sons of the living God -- Hosea 1:10

24. That by him, and through him, and of him the worlds are and were created, and the inhabitants thereof are begotten sons and daughters unto God. -- D&C 76:24

Miracles Are Wrought By Faith, And Angels Appear To Minister Unto Men

25. Wherefore, by the ministering of angels, and by every word which proceeded forth out of the mouth of God, men began to exercise faith in Christ; and thus by faith, they did lay hold upon every good thing; and thus it was until the coming of Christ.

26. And after that he came men also were saved by faith in his name; and by faith, they become the sons of God. And as surely as Christ liveth he spake these words unto our fathers, saying: Whatsoever thing ye shall ask the Father in my name, which is good, in faith believing that ye shall receive, behold, it shall be done unto you.

27. Wherefore, my beloved brethren, have miracles ceased because Christ hath ascended into heaven, and hath sat down on the right hand of God, to claim of

the Father his rights of mercy which he hath upon the children of men?

28. For he hath answered the ends of the law, and he claimeth all those who have faith in him; and they who have faith in him will cleave unto every good thing wherefore he advocateth the cause of the children of men; and he dwelleth eternally in the heavens.

29. And because he hath done this, my beloved brethren, have miracles ceased? Behold I say unto you Nay; neither have angels ceased to minister unto the children of men.

30. For behold, they are subject unto him, to minister according to the word of his command, showing themselves unto them of strong faith and a firm mind in every form of godliness...

36. Or have angels ceased to appear unto the children of men? Or has he withheld the power of the Holy Ghost from them? Or will he, so long as time shall last, or the earth shall stand, or there shall be one man upon the face thereof to be saved?

37. Behold I say unto you, Nay; for it is by faith that miracles are wrought; and it is by faith that angels appear and minister unto men; wherefore, if these things have ceased, wo be unto the children of men,

for it is because of unbelief, and all is vain.

-- Moroni 7:25-30, 36-37

Without your faith working, the Lord can do nothing. You are an important part of life. The Lord works through us, through our Faith, our righteous desires and waits for us to awaken to our power, then links his power up to our prayers of faith. On every occasion when the Prophet Joseph Smith received revelation, he first had to ask. He desired to know. We have to ask first to receive also.

Alma knew of this principle and knew that when we could awaken the sleeping giant of Faith within us, that the mysteries of God would open up to us. Is not the power of the Law Of Faith not a mystery of God, one that we are supposed to unlock? When the missionary force and the body of the church are able to use this great faith, and be of one mind and one heart in our prayers of faith, then thousands, even millions of souls will come unto Christ and the Restored Gospel. Our Faith must now be awakened. We are the generation the Lord is waiting to work with. Let us Do It!

To Him Who Repents And Asks With Faith In Christ Are Things Revealed Which Never Have Been Revealed Before

22. Yea, he that repenteth and exerciseth faith, and
bringeth forth good works, and prayeth continually
without ceasing—unto such it is given to know the
mysteries of God; yea, unto such it shall be given to
reveal things which never have been revealed; yea, and
it shall be given unto such to bring thousands of souls

to repentance, even as it has been given unto us to bring these our brethren to repentance. -- Alma 26:22

This promise is unto all who are of great faith.

Your Faith In Jesus Christ Overcomes The World
4. For whatsoever is born of God overcometh the world [wicked]: and this is the victory that overcometh the world, even our faith.

5. Who is he that overcometh the world, but he that believeth that Jesus is the Son of God? -- 1 John 5:4-5

Learn To Have Faith

This then is the challenge. It is yours and mine to learn how to USE that Faith which Doubts Not. This is it – that we know that Jesus Christ lives, and with that faith overcome the world. WE are as the armies of Helaman who were taught in their youth. They had the complete faith to overcome. And by that faith they did overcome.

Each of us also have that power within us. You and I are as a sleeping giant. We are the Lord's army who will learn to awaken our dormant powers of Faith, for we know that Jesus Christ Lives, and We Doubt Not this great truth. Wherefore, our confirmed righteous desires will come to pass. Let us not use this great knowledge to get worldly possessions beyond our needs, but use these truths to become Pure In Heart and spread the Gospel of Jesus Christ over the earth. Let us prepare for the Millennium should it come in our time.

We CAN overcome this world. We CAN become pure and return to live with our PURE Heavenly Parents through the Son. This I know, in the name of Jesus Christ, Amen.

Sincerely,
Carolyn Pearce Ringger July 4, 2013

ABOUT THE AUTHOR

I felt it important that I introduce myself so that you would understand the circumstances under which *Faith Unpuzzled, Reaching Toward Heaven (Covenant Publications 1992)* and *My Life Is A JOY To Me* programs came into being. Neither program was premeditated or pre-planned by me in the sense that I set out deliberately to prepare such a plan for publication. Rather, they grew spontaneously out of a need in my own life, when I sought the Lord's help in meeting and mastering that need. I felt myself being led in all the things that I have done.

This material has helped me to meet and overcome problems in my own life. I know that it can also help you in yours, because it is based on true principles of faith as found in the scriptures and in messages from our leaders.

The materials which I present here are not a part of any formal church program, nor are they intended as such. Rather, they are simply the answers which I was given for my own personal and family use, which worked for us. However, since I originally put the materials together, many others have asked me to share with them, and they also found it to be of value in helping them in their own lives. I have been invited to speak from California to Maryland, from Canada to Mexico, and many have told me afterward how valuable the materials have been for them in their lives.

Understanding The Laws Of Faith Came Slowly

Learning to understand and use the Laws of Faith came as a slow difficult process which extended over many years. Indeed, these insights came as a direct outgrowth of meeting life's many challenges. I would like to invite you to accompany me now as I recall those years, of walking through our trials and share with you the insights and understandings which came to me as a result of those experiences.

1976 was the year when I first came truly face to face with life's challenges and realized that I must meet them and learn. I was a young mother at home during those years, with a very hard working, and caring husband. We had five active young children, filling our lives with their demands, ages eight to six months. We had just moved to Mesa, Arizona two years before from Orem, Utah, where my husband had recently completed his master's degree at BYU in Mechanical Engineering. We had loved our four years of University life with our new and growing babies. Those were happier, easier years and now we were in Phoenix with a job at Garrett Turbine Engine Co.

I was an eager and deeply concerned young mother. I wanted the best for my sweetheart and our five children, as well as for myself. I had a deep commitment to help bring this about in all of our lives. I had never had any other aspirations really, beyond that, other than to find joy and help my family find joy through understanding and living the commandments of God, and to grow and become happier.

My childhood and youth had been most fulfilled and happy. I had learned through the excellent example and love of my parents, Don and Eileen Pearce, how to love and serve others. There was another deeply important influence also which I had during my teen years that of our MIA Girl's Camp, called Camp Shalom, in the Mt. Rubidoux Stake in Riverside, California. Each summer we would go up and spend one to two weeks, learning to relate to ourselves, each other, and to our Heavenly Father.

My experience, first as a young camper and then later as

camp leader over the younger girls, gave me faith in myself, and a deep, abiding testimony and conviction that I would live a clean life full of service. Our stake offered shadow leadership to help the girls learn how to become future stake camp directors. I had the experience of stake camp leadership at ages 17-18 in California and at age 19-20 in Hawaii serving as their first Stake Camp Director. It was the marvelous effect of the Pine Cone Ceremony which year by year had purified my soul.

We would take a pine cone to represent a bad habit, throw it into the fire, and watch it burn in the glowing embers as we replaced it with a chosen good habit. I could literally *feel* the Spirit there at Girl's Camp. It was the sisterhood I felt there, with the campfire glowing, ukuleles humming, and the harmony of the girls' voices as they sang which touched my soul. These experiences helped me to firm up my determination to always follow the Spirit of truth, and a deep testimony began to grow. I decided then that I would keep my thoughts pure and follow the commandments. I would love and serve others and keep myself free of the sins of the world.

Because my real self was set in place by my parents, the LDS Church's standards and teachings plus the MIA Girls' Camp, I was able to recognize what to do when the trials of real life began to hit us.

All Marriages Will Be Tried – Spoiler Seeks To Destroy That Greatest Of All Units, The Family!

I remember having thoughts come into my mind at one period of our life, which were totally foreign to my nature. They went something like this; "You don't like your situation. Marriage is not as easy as you thought it would be.

You are supposed to be happy just because you are married, but now you know that this isn't so. Why don't you leave!"

But then from deep inside of me came the response, "NO! I will not leave just because I discovered that life is hard at times!" What happened to the deep love I felt for my cute husband when we were first married? The Spirit of the Lord had confirmed that he was the right one to marry. What is going on? I have heard that love does have a way of changing into something deeper. I desire for it to grow not go. I need help Father. These thoughts are not mine! (I have since learned that just because the Spirit gives you a confirmation, it is not saying that we will have a perfect marriage. It is stating that you are two Pure In Heart beings who get to work together!)

Then I felt the Spirit's instruction within my mind teaching me that in order to destroy the children's home foundation, the evil one must first destroy the relationship of the parents. That meant *my sweetheart and I* are the ones they will attack first to get to our children. I remember looking at the pictures of our five wonderful children and making a mental decision, "No evil force is going to get these kids. The Lord has given us this stewardship and I will do whatever is necessary to strengthen our marriage in order to help these five most important children in our lives. I will teach them to be pure in heart so that they can return to our Heavenly Father." I love my husband, I love our children and I will not allow difficulties to be resolved in the way of the world! No way! Father help me, I am confused. Wilt thou teach me? How do I do my part to create a Happier Marriage?"

I had thought before that joy was a natural side-effect of being married in the temple and living the commandments.

But then I had never had to deal with a man as a husband before. My father had always dealt with me in such a different way, as a sweet, young, talented daughter. He gave me praise and made me feel that I could do anything. My husband, though, didn't know of my needs. He had never been a husband before and didn't know the needs of his wife. The same goes for me. I had never been a wife before and I did not know the needs of a husband. I guess what I wanted was more of what I was used to. I had to go through a time of depression to awaken me. I was an adult now, not a daughter in the home, and should be able to fill my own well of happiness, by using the laws of faith in Jesus Christ, and improved self-image, more positive inner self-talk and better spouse communication.

How amazing it is that we actually think that as long as we pay our tithing, go on a mission, marry in the Temple, and live the commandments that happiness automatically will be ours. I have since learned that it isn't marriage which makes people happy. Rather, it's Happy People who make Happy Marriages. I learned that I needed to correct something within myself. False expectations of what a husband should be like along with errors in my self-image were causing me hurt until I learned *how* to correct them. I learned *how* to watch over my thoughts so that they would express what I desired in my marriage and home. And as I did my marriage and home life began to show the fruits of my change of self-talk. I also called upon the Lord to soften both my heart and my husband's, that he might also desire to change, and listen more fully to the whisperings of the Spirit to know of my needs. You cannot make a man change. The natural man gets in the way. So, ask the Lord to work with him. After all, your husband is His Father's son. What a fascinating experience! Suddenly I realized that *I was* living the law of faith! *I was* hoping for things that I could not see, which is how FAITH works.

Marriage is a real challenge, and the evil one uses everything in his power to destroy the family unit. Whenever the couple is weak, they will be tried. The home where the husband and wife are of one heart and one mind with the Lord is the greatest unit in the universe, and since we have the potential of becoming this most powerful unit under the Lord, who would want to destroy it? The Spoiler, of course.

Bombarded By Evil Thoughts

My testing was not over. Later that year there was a destructive three months when I went through a constant bombardment of evil thoughts. Where were these thoughts coming from? I knew these terrible ideas were not mine. Yet they came to me in my own tone of voice, as though they were my own. These immoral thoughts would descend upon me, then taunt me, telling me I was a hypocrite. And I would say; "No, I will not live these filthy thoughts. They are not mine!"

Then a wonderful thing happened. A new neighbor moved in down the street. As we became acquainted, I learned that she had been a missionary in my home town of Glen Avon, California, 13 miles west of Riverside. She was there while I was away to BYU my freshman year.

While we were getting acquainted I asked her if she knew the Terrill family. Yes, she said she did. In fact she had been one of the missionaries who had brought about Brother Terrill's baptism. He joined the church while I was away, and became very active. I had always desired to know the story behind his conversion. She said that the Spirit taught them that he knew that the Gospel was true; he just needed to be asked to join. They listened to and courageously followed the Still Small Voice. Then they challenged him to be baptized. They set a date and told him that the font would be full of warm water. The Elders would also be there dressed in white ready to baptize him.

The Sister's actions in challenging him brought about an upheaval from the realms of darkness, though. She said that one night just two or three days before the scheduled baptism, they were awakened by a spirit of darkness which was standing at the foot of their bed. He complained that they were intruding on his area, and told them to stay out of it. The Sisters' response was to phone the Elders and have them come and pronounce a blessing over their area to cast out the evil spirit. That blessing had its desired effect in protecting them and their work, and Brother Terrill arrived safely at his baptism.

As I listened to Jo Ann Boyd's story I suddenly recognized that all these ugly thoughts which I had been experiencing had come from the same kind of evil influence, which was trying to intrude on my area. It came to me then that I too needed a priesthood blessing, to help rid me of the evil thoughts which were trying to influence me. It took two blessings over the next three months to work through that trying time. I learned then of the destructive power which the evil one can exert in our lives, whispering in our ear the messages of hate, fear, anger, racism and filth, as 2 Nephi 28:20-22 tries to describe.

That's what had been happening to me over the past three months. Those thoughts were not mine. They had been planted there by the Spoiler, and because I hadn't recognized that they were directly from him, I didn't know how to combat them, and had allowed them to remain. But I could exert control and command them to leave.

That was a lesson I never forgot. For the first time I became aware that we can receive messages from the spirit of darkness, though it was a year or two later before I finally realized how we also receive messages likewise from the Beings of Light. I also realized at that time that we can talk to our thoughts, because they are always talking to us.

Another thing I realized during this time was that Satan tries especially hard to destroy those who might have been endowed with a special calling. A friend told me about how her father, when he was made a Patriarch, had been tried by doubting thoughts concerning the gospel's truthfulness. I wasn't aware at that time that I might have a special calling, but Satan knows, and he uses that knowledge to seek to destroy us.

That year of 1976 was one of my most challenging years. But I was yet to receive further testing before things began to brighten and become better. I was feeling exhausted from all this stress, and so for my birthday the following October, I felt that I needed a chance to get away by myself to rest and be around my parents and sisters. I went to visit my folks up in American Fork for a week and while I was there I learned that one of my brothers had also been bombarded by the temptations of Satan and was fooled, falling into the evil thoughts of the natural man put into the mind by 'The Spoiler'. As I learned about the trials he was walking through, I knew immediately HOW it could happen for I had been under attack and survived. I was up there to heal from my own spiritual wounds.

I had learned that there are two radio-like stations transmitting messages to us all of the time, one from LIGHT and the other from DARKNESS. It was during this time that I realized I needed to prepare some materials to help my family and others, to give them the benefit of what I had learned during my time of trial. I had survived. Now it was time for me to reach out and help others. The material I compiled at that time became the foundation material for my first book, My Life Is A JOY To Me, which was published in 1984.

I Learned How The Lord Speaks Into Our Mind

1978 was an especially hard year. It seemed like everything was happening to us. My husband was diagnosed as having cancer and was given a 60-40 percent chance to live, though to me it seemed like it was really 50-50. I was frightened. Hans had a first exploratory surgery and was to go in now for his second operation. We were all fasting and praying and I called family members in Canada, Utah, Colorado, and Virginia to fast and pray with us. We also had asked our Bishop, Dick Skousen, and Elders Quorum President, Jim Jamieson, to come and administer to him. Jim was to be the mouthpiece.

Then the first beautiful miracle occurred. My husband was told that he would be made well and whole, and as I sat there listening, the marvelous confirmation of the Spirit came over me, the tingling and burning sensation which D&C 9:8 explains. It enveloped my whole being and I *knew* that everything would be all right. I *knew* that he would be healed and made whole.

However, troubles still continued to plague us. The hot water heater broke, the roof started to leak, and that alone would require $300 to fix. The garbage disposal went out, and even the sewer line collapsed. Under this next stressful situation another miracle occurred. I felt the heavy burden of depression upon me every moment; the trials were more than I could bear. I had asked for the trials to stop, that I could stand no more. Yet my request did not stop them. I retired to my prayer room; it was no longer just the bedroom. I poured out my heart to the Lord of all, and explained how I realized that asking for the trials to stop didn't work. I now asked for something else. "Wilt thou please take from me the deep sorrow I have felt? Wilt thou take the weight from my tired shoulders, the stress and tears that have flowed too easily?"

It was then, when I asked for that which the Lord would grant, that in an instant all depression, all sorrow was taken from me and I knew peace. I know that God lives and answers prayers. I know how the people in Mosiah 24:10-17 must have felt. Their trials did not cease, yet they carried their burdens and did not feel them. Said the Lord:

> 14. And I will also ease the burdens which are put upon your shoulders, *that even you cannot feel them upon your backs,* even while you are in bondage; and this will I do that ye may stand as witnesses for me hereafter, and that ye may know of a surety that I, the Lord God, do visit my people in their afflictions. -- Mosiah 24:14

We Need To Get Away To A Cabin

After my husband's third operation, this time for gallstones instead of cancer, I felt I couldn't take it anymore, and again I sent a call for help to the Lord. I felt that my reserves had run dry, I had no more to give. I felt an urgent need to get away with my sweetheart for awhile from the continuing pressure of children's needs and demands. As I sat thinking on the couch one day I allowed my own real needs and desires to flow forth, even though I was sure there was no earthly way to receive it. "We need to get away," I said to myself. I don't know whether I spoke it silently or out loud. But I know I heard a voice spoken in reply, which I heard within myself. It said, "Yes, you need to get away."

I knew I was alone, yet I heard a voice, just above me and to the right, spoken into my mind and sort of in my own tone of voice. Yet I knew it was someone else talking.

What a welcome change. Someone was agreeing with me. I thought, "I don't know who you are but let's keep talking." It spoke; "You need to get away to a cabin," "A cabin?" I thought, "We can't afford to rent a cabin." "Just tell someone," the voice responded, "and it will be so."

It was less than a half an hour after that when a friend called me on the phone to ask me how I was. We talked for a while then she asked me if I needed anything. The inner voice said to share with her what I had been told so I did. I replied, "We need to get away to a cabin." She replied that she had a friend who had a cabin to rent and perhaps she had an opening. Mentally I said; "Spirit, I thought this was going to be free." We had no money left after paying the expenses and doctor bills. I thanked her for her thoughtfulness, we chatted some more then hung up.

Not long after that Carole Augustin, my visiting teacher, stopped by to drop off a much needed item, a strictly voluntary gesture on her part. As we chatted she too asked me if there was anything we needed. Oh, I thought, I am not going to use the word cabin again, but I will say this, "We need to get away." Her eyes sparkled; "Oh, we have a cabin up on Mt. Graham," she said. "You can leave tomorrow and stay as long as you would like." Then the inner thought intruded, "but what will we do with the kids?" and as though she had read my thoughts she added, "And I'll take care of the kids!"

What joy and gratitude I felt. I could hardly believe what I had just heard. The Lord had spoken into my mind and then granted us my desire. I began to truly understand that there are beings helping us, whom we cannot see. They know our very thoughts and can talk to us through our thoughts when we turn to them for help. We must learn faith, to hope for things we do not see. They speak to our spirits, as though we had no body. Joseph Smith wrote regarding this:

> All things whatsoever God in his infinite wisdom has seen fit and proper to reveal to us, while we are dwelling in mortality, in regard to our mortal bodies, are revealed to us in the abstract, and independent of affinity of this mortal tabernacle, but are revealed to our spirits precisely as though we had no bodies at all... *Teachings Of The Prophet Joseph Smith*, pg. 355

It was around this time that I began to understand more of the meaning of the scriptures. I began to see things in the scriptures which I had hardly noticed or understood before. And as I studied, certain passages jumped off the page as the meaning became clear to my understanding. Why, they may have been written hundreds or even thousands of years ago but they were written for me today just as surely as they had been for those for whom they were originally written. And through the Holy Ghost I was beginning to understand their meaning and how they applied to me today.

It was during this time that I began listening more fully

to the spirit's promptings. And as I did I began to change. I found I was having better communication with my husband. I learned to become strong. Women are not a doormat and neither are they the boss. There is a fine balance in between. And how do we find that balance? By listening to the Spirit. Listening in this way I have learned to discern the difference between positive and negative promptings. The question is not, "Is it true or false?" but rather, "Is it constructive or destructive?" a statement can be true and still be destructive. For instance, the thought I'd had, "You and your husband are so different" was true. But men and women are different. But that difference can serve to strengthen rather than undermine a marriage if used properly. I have a friend and I have also known of others who decided that they should divorce simply because they did think differently. If they could have only realized that it was the Spoiler talking, to undermine their marriage and destroy their home.

Send The Children To Utah

Let me share with you another situation which occurred also during this difficult time. We needed to have the children get away while the radiation treatments were going on. The instruction was placed in my mind to talk to members of the Relief Society Stake Board where I was serving as a member, and tell them of our need, and it would be granted. I did. I called a few members and told them, and within 24 hours four of the five children were gone, staying with their grandparents in Utah, and we were freed from that stress. Our youngest, Hans, stayed with us.

Even Plants Matter To The Lord If They Matter To Me

Even little things matter! I desired some plants for our home. I began to see where I could even ask for them. "Father, is it ok to have some plants for our home? There is no money in the budget for them." A wife's self-image deals with how the home looks but the husband's way of thinking needs money in the bank to protect the family's unseen needs. And the Spirit said, "Yes. It's all right to ask for plants." So I wrote down "We have green plants," on my desire list. I presented it to the Lord in my prayers and doubted not. I knew that it would come about because the Spirit said it was ok.

One day the instruction came to my mind, "Go to Frys' Grocery Store." My first thought was, "I don't want to go to Frys'." The inner instructions came again, "Go to Frys'." Finally I recognized the thoughts as positive, pure and enlightening. Therefore they were instructions from the Spirit. So I went to Frys' and looked around for the reason I had been sent there. Then I spied a number of plants on the floor, Philodendron, which looked rather yellow. I knew water would bring them back. My next impression was that they were going to be marked down, "Go talk to the manager," the inner voice said, so I followed the instructions. I asked him if they were going to mark them down? "Yes," he said, "How much would you like to pay for them?" I bought some plants for a dollar each, my constant reminder that the Lord loves me and that my small desires really do matter to Him.

This is marvelous. Even plants matter to the Lord if they matter to me. So I started writing down the things we needed, a couch, a chest of drawers, anything we needed I wrote down and presented to the Lord and asked if it was for our good? The Spirit would confirm, and time after time our needs were fulfilled at a price we could afford to pay. Each day I would ask only for those items we needed. Then I would thank him throughout the day that it would be coming to pass. And if doubting thoughts came I would talk to them and tell them to leave.

I Desired To Learn What Is A Self-Image

It was shortly after this time when I was told by a man, whom I was selling an Aloe Vera product under, that to do better I would apparently need to improve my self-image. I worked hard with little progress. He taught me that I could not climb any higher in my sales, than my self-image would allow me to. What did he mean? I decided to pray and receive the help I needed to understand. "Father," I asked, "I hurt. What is a self-image? What is controlling my life that I do not understand?" I prayed for Light and Knowledge on this new topic. As I studied, pondered and prayed, the Holy Ghost began to enlarge my understanding, and I began to gain a most awesome picture of the human personality.

I learned about the brain and how we program it by the thoughts which we think. I discovered how by talking to my thoughts I can erase negative thoughts and replace them with positive thoughts. I found I could program my brain to forgive myself and others and that is when I programmed I Erase and Replace. (Also found later at the end of Lesson #3.) I was a horrible procrastinator too, so I programmed Persistence for myself. I wanted to grow in my marriage so I created and programmed, "Marriage Is A JOY To Me," for all to strengthen their own marriages.

All of the affirmations I have written to help individuals strengthen themselves, can be found in our programming book and CD's called, MY LIFE IS A JOY TO ME. I wanted to have and to live by the whole picture and to strengthen the whole person, the body, mind, and spirit. Gradually I pieced all these things together, and programmed them into my brain-servant.

I developed *Faith Unpuzzled* and *My Life Is A JOY To Me* programs, to help me solve the problems in my own life. These are marvelous concepts! They worked for me and they will work for anyone who will use them, because they are built on true principles.

I learned that when I lie down to rest, and program an affirmation, that it goes into my subconscious and is accepted by my brain-servant to become a part of me. I am not my brain nor am I my body. I am spirit inside of this physical body. My spirit intelligence is the thinking part of me. The brain is a servo-mechanism, attracting to me my most persistent thoughts.

I Started Teaching A Class

Then later, as I shared these concepts with a friend, I was asked if I would teach a class in her store on how to overcome Self-Defeating Behaviors. I formulated eight lessons. The first lesson I created from the materials I had researched on the brain, how it operates, and how we can correct the way we talk to ourselves to erase negative thoughts and pattern our servant, the brain, to become more productive in helping us become a happier person. We must improve our self-image, which forms the roots of our life, by changing our inner self-talk. Thus we change the fruits or results of life. Thought is matter and we attract what we keep thinking about.

Some of the class members then asked me if I would give my first lesson on "How To Turn Life's Negative Into

Positives" in their Relief Society. By the time I had given the talk in two or three wards, I began to receive requests from all over the state and then from other states. The real reason for the success of this material, I feel, is that I am a mother at home. I was seeking help for real problems that women at home face daily. This material answered the real needs of the listeners. A person who has a good self-image has a real power or light within, the power of faith, which links with our testimony of Jesus Christ, and allows us to dig in and solve the problem.

As I taught how to improve one's own self-image and How To Turn Life's Negatives Into Positives, my own mental eyes were gradually opened. I began to realize how my faith was connected to my watching over my own thoughts, and it was at this point that I studied out and put together the Faith Unpuzzled materials.

I started in 1981 to share what I had learned, giving about 25 talks a year. Then the request grew to 55 talks per year. All of our materials have the theme of *My Life Is A JOY To Me.* Like a great flower unfolding, this *Faith Unpuzzled* Program has grown out of the first talk on how to become happy as a wife and mother in the home.

As I asked for light and further knowledge, on faith, read my scriptures, I began to see the words heart and faith on every page. I highlighted these words each time and like a path unfolding, I could see that the laws of faith were everywhere and that I had been using them in solving my problems. This gracious experience brings about the fulfillment of part of my Patriarchal Blessing. I was told that I would play a *vital* part in helping my brothers and sisters in the church, that many will be led to bless and thank me for the influence I have had in their lives. Giving talks and preparing the materials, which have been selling for over 28 years, has made this sweet experience come to pass. I love people. I love our Heavenly Father and His Son, Jesus Christ, for the Pure Beings that they are. I honor their ways and I desire to become pure even as they are pure, by watching over my thoughts one day at a time.

The scriptures feel like "Letters from Home", from a real Father. And his Son, Jesus Christ, began to feel more like my big brother who set a good example for me to follow. Jesus had prepared the way for us so we could get back HOME to the Father of us all. Earth is not our beginning; earth life is our test. The scriptures are letters to us on *how* to get back home to live, with the beings of purity and light. The scriptures also are "Lectures on Faith" or reports showing *how* others solved their problems by using the *Law Of Faith* as taught to them by the Father.

Because I ask for more **Light And Knowledge** about Faith, you now have that research in your hands. This book is the third rewrite of that material. Light and Knowledge comes to anyone who will ask and doubt not. My experiences are living proof of that principle. It has blessed not only me and my family but others in growing numbers as well, as the way has been opened for me to share it with them. I feel this program is blessed of the Lord, and I feel most grateful that through it I can serve as an instrument in helping others create their own happiness with the help of the Lord.

Here Is What Faith Means To Me Now

Faith to me now means that the following truths are firmly set in my soul, 1) I know that Jesus Christ lives. 2) I Doubt Him Not. 3) All things are possible through Christ.

4) Therefore, whatsoever I shall ask of the Father, in the name of Christ, it shall be granted me after it is confirmed by the Holy Ghost that it is for my good. (Mormon 9:18-21, Moroni 7:20-28, D&C 46:7, 30) I know we can be blessed with whatever we need. Realize therefore that whatever keeps coming into your mind and weighing upon your thoughts, which is pure, is of the Holy Ghost. (See D&C 128:1 ... subject seems to occupy my mind, and press itself upon my feelings the strongest ...) This is the area in your life to be working on.

We have written down our family's desires for our needs and missionary sons, Eric and Kevin, and had them confirmed by the Spirit of truth. Then when the Spirit confirms the request, we know that it is now God's will and will come to pass by our faith. We hope for things we do not see, use our mental effort to stay single-minded, and walk on the path of faith. And by that faith in Jesus Christ, we are able to overcome all things.

What a humbling reality this all is. Our sorrows, our trials, our temptations have all turned to *JOY* and we want for nothing, just as James 1:2-8 describes. When we are single-minded, we receive from the Lord.

Washington D.C. – With Our Son

In 1986 I had a great experience at Mt. Vernon while I was in Washington D.C. with our son, Eric. He had just graduated from high school, and was receiving the Presidential Scholar Award on the White House lawn, along with selected students from each of the other states.

When Eric's award was made known to us, I desired with my whole soul to be able to go see him and to be there in such a once-in-a-lifetime experience. I pondered over how I could use my faith to help my desire come to pass. I had been invited six months earlier by Bunny Whitney, owner of the bookstore, This Is The Place, which is located in the Washington Temple area, to come and speak on my materials. But so far nothing had worked out. I decided to ask her what she thought about the idea of her paying one third of the travel expense and also allowing me to stay at her home, thus the miracle of being able to see Eric at the White House could also be brought about.

I went in sincere prayer to the Lord and asked Him if this was okay. The Spirit confirmed my request. I then prayed, and presented to the Lord what I needed to have this miracle come about. After I finished praying, I immediately called Bunny.

Ring ... ring ... "Hello," Ah, she was home. "This is Carolyn Ringger," I said, "calling from Mesa, Arizona." Excitement came into her voice. We were finally talking about how I might get out there to Maryland to speak. I explained my situation to her, how our son was receiving an award in Washington, and that I would love to fulfill her request and be able to see him at the same time.

She immediately caught the idea and started to explain to me how she thought it could work. I asked her if she felt good about the idea of her paying one third of the plane ticket? "Oh, yes," she replied, and she extended to me also the invitation to stay at her home. She would house me and drive me to the White House each day and generally care for a visitor's needs. An inexpressible JOY filled my heart. My request had been brought to pass through the help of those unseen Beings of Light. We cannot see them yet they are there to help us if we but ask in faith. "Oh thank you! And thank you, Bunny, for allowing the use of all my sales materials to finish paying for the trip. You are indeed a great kindred spirit." I have found Bunny's kind of greatness wherever I have been asked to speak.

I was able, therefore, to go see Eric and to experience with him this great event in his life. To see President Reagan and to *feel* the spirit of our country there on the grounds of the White House, with all of its history, caused my soul to overflow with new Joy. These are the fruits of life which we should enjoy. There was no way I was going to allow this chance to pass me by. But to make these things come to pass takes faith and effort. Nothing happens by accident. I was there because someone desired for me to come, and to share what I had learned in the MY LIFE IS A JOY TO ME materials. I could not have gone otherwise. I know that the Lord was watching over me. The blessings I have had because I followed the righteous desires in my heart in creating materials to help others, are more than I could have ever imagined.

Our many trials really had fine-tuned my spirit. Now I could hear and follow promptings in normal day-to-day life instead of just calling upon the Lord in a crisis. It was in the writings of Moroni that I learned how to lay hold on every good thing. He teaches;

20. And now, my brethren, how is it possible that ye can lay hold upon every good thing?

21. And now I come to that faith, of which I said I would speak; and I will tell you the way whereby ye may lay hold on every good thing.

25. ...men began to exercise faith in Christ; and thus

by faith, they did lay hold upon every good thing; and thus it was until the coming of Christ.

26. And after that he came men also were saved by faith in his name; and by faith, they become the sons of God. And as surely as Christ liveth he spake these words unto our fathers, saying: Whatsoever thing ye shall ask the Father in my name, which is good, in faith believing that ye shall receive, behold, it shall be done unto you. -- Moroni 7:20-28

The Lord Answered My Prayer At Mount Vernon

I want to tell you about what happened at Mt. Vernon on the second day. The students' time was being fully taken up, so the parents were free to tour the historic sights of the area. I desired to go and visit Mt. Vernon, where I could tread the lanes of history and walk the same paths where George Washington walked. I crossed the acres of his old estate, past the carriage house, the smoke house, and the velvet-green pastures where horses trotted yet. I stood and watched through wooden fences as these gracious animals hastened past. I love seeing their manes flow freely in the breeze, and the rippling of their muscles as they galloped.

I had a question, though, upon which I needed to receive an answer. I could feel the Spirit close to me as I asked, "Lord, am I doing what thou wouldst have me do? As I go out to share what thou hast taught me about the laws of faith, and how to help people create more *JOY* in their lives - I have to leave our home to speak. There are many times when my family says I should stop speaking and stay home. Am I doing what thou wouldst have me do?"

I pondered, listening for the Still Small Voice of the Spirit to come, as it had done before, to give me an answer. I knew that I had to ask and continue to ask until I received a definite answer. I continued to walk, pondering deeply. I felt the total sense of history there at Mt. Vernon, with its two hundred year-old home, its sloping paths meandered down to the shores of the Potomac River then back to the tombs of George and Martha Washington.

Again and again I asked, "Dear Lord of all the universe, am I doing what thou wouldst have me do? Am I doing what is thy will? If it isn't thy will I will stop giving talks." I knew that the talks I was giving were not to gratify my own pride. Rather, I was sharing, by the request of others, who had acted by the impressions they received from the Spirit. This material was causing others to understand scriptural truths which had puzzled the minds of many. I could see that the material was awakening a sleeping giant within the people who heard the presentations. I was told after each talk, audience after audience, that lives had been changed. One person said he decided not to commit suicide after hearing *Faith Unpuzzled*. Another said she realized that she should not get a divorce and leave her family. Missionaries had written and explained that the simple concepts we presented, helped them learn how to use the Laws Of Faith, to the extent that they were able to ask and receive the righteous desires of their hearts, finding people to teach and baptize.

I am but one person, but I *can* make a difference. I *can* see that this is real. As I teach each correct principle, the listeners are able to understand the plain truths, and to better govern themselves. That is how we can bind the Spoiler in preparation for the Millennium. I deeply desire to help stop the filth from flooding the land I love, and to help faith, and the fruits of righteous desires, to flood our cities, our towns, our families, and our hearts. We each need to learn how we can become pure in heart, and to cleanse the inner vessel, as President Benson has challenged us to do.

As I passed Washington's home to my left, with its acres of green lawns, walking toward the Potomac, I exerted my faith with all my might, and cried again to Him within my heart. "Father, am I doing thy will? I ask thee in the name of thy Son, Jesus Christ." It was then that I heard the familiar Still Small Voice, the one who taught me on the couch when we needed to get away, the voice which spoke to tell me to call my friends on the Stake Board to find a ride for the kids and it was so. This was the voice I desired to hear again. It did speak to my spirit as if I had no body for it comes into the mind as thoughts. All this came about through great mental effort.

"Yes, my dear daughter," it said, "You are doing what I would have you do." Then it continued, "Please turn around and look toward the home. Now look at the two towering, giant trees on your left. Those trees were planted over 200 years ago by the Washington family. They were just tiny seedlings when they were planted, yet look at the size and strength of them now. They are giant trees of great strength."

The Spirit continued, "You, my dear daughter, are planting seeds also of knowledge of the laws of Faith and *how* they can work. Then, just as these huge trees have grown, so shall the seeds of knowledge which you are now planting, grow and increase in the earth."

Tears of Joy filled my eyes and rolled down my cheeks, for again I *knew* that I was doing what our Father in Heaven would have me do. I am a wife and mother at home, one with a message learned from the Lord, after the trials we have walked through, individually and as a family. I must use wisdom. I must balance my time to see that my husband's and family's needs come first, then allow this quiet mission to speak to those who ask.

Closing Thoughts

Some have asked me, "Who gave you the authority to speak?" No one other than the Spirit. But into my mind always comes the scriptural passage found in D&C 58:26-27;

26. For behold, it is not meet that I should command in all things; for he that is compelled in all things, the same is a slothful and not a wise servant; wherefore he receiveth no reward.

27. Verily I say, man (and women) should be anxiously engaged in a good cause, and do many things of their own free will, and bring to pass much righteousness;

When I speak I offer it of my own free will to those who are seeking help. I ask the Lord to put my name into the minds of Ward, Stake and Mission leaders. They follow through on this pure thought, and call to set up a time for me to speak. They pay just for my travel or flight expenses. I have been told time and time again by these leaders that they had been prompted to ask me to come. I have also received letters from many who have benefited from this material. Who am I to say no to the Lord when my brothers and sisters call and share with me their impressions from the Spirit?

How Do You Do It?

Sometimes people ask me, "How do you do it? It seems so easy for you." But it wasn't easy, believe me. I was simply determined that I would have *JOY*. I had experienced joy in my youth in our home and especially through girl's camp. It was this outside exposure at camp which helped seal the training I had received at home. I decided while I was still in my early teens that I wanted to have peace and joy in my life. I wanted to help people. Often during my high school years I would wonder, "How will we bind Satan for the Millennium?" Whenever I ran into filth, I would ask in my mind, "How are we going to stop it? How are we going to bind him?" I studied the scriptures on this topic. I thought upon it in my mind and heart for years, and pondered and prayed over it.

It was during our trials as adults that I came to understand the meaning of the word, "heart" as it is used in the scriptures. Most often it means, "Thoughts in the mind." (Ensign, July 1984, p. 31) Then one day a great comprehension swept over me on how we can stop Satan in part. Because we will listen to him no more in our mind and heart and thoughts. (Institute Manual, 1985-86, p.89)

I knew what it was like to be under attack. I had experienced it myself, and Apostle Marriner W. Merrill had also described it in an incident that happened to him at the Logan Temple, which was quoted in Lesson #5, where Satan threatened to stop temple work from being done. He whispers in people's ears, tempting them. But we have a safeguard. James 4:7 tells us, "Resist the devil and he will flee from you."

I decided that I would take James for exactly what he said. So I told those evil thoughts that they may not stay. I will not allow impure thoughts to remain in my mind. It is a daily effort. My most effective way to handle impure thoughts is to say, "I delete you!"

Each day I ask for angels and for the shield of purity to cover me. The shield is real, like a glass dome, it is spiritual, and it is something I can mentally see. I visualize it. And whenever the attacking thoughts try to start, I say, "Father, by my faith in Jesus Christ, I ask for Thy protective shield of purity to cover me, and for angels to attend me, to keep me from impure thoughts. I know that thy Son liveth, and I doubt Him not. Father, I know what impurity is, and I want to surround myself with pure things, -- with pure music and pure thoughts, and able to live with pure beings."

My greatest desire is that Faith may flood the land instead of filth. And that Satan shall be bound, that we listen to him no more in our hearts or thoughts. I may be but one person but I know that I am making a difference, just as my patriarchal blessing expressed saying that I will play a *vital role*. That was a word that had no particular meaning for me at the time it was given. It wasn't until 1986 that I even noticed it. Then later, as I began to receive letters from those who had been helped, I could see what was beginning to happen. I desire with all of my soul, to Awaken the Sleeping Giant within all who may come in contact with this material.

What if we can thereby help cause faith like unto that of Enoch's to flood the land. What a choice mission these trials would have awakened me to. I honor the magnificent, pure-in-heart beings in our universe whom I serve, and I love the fruits of truths they teach. I know that I can simply and sincerely ask for more Light and Knowledge on the Laws of Faith and receive it. We can each receive the miraculous results of such personal revelation. It is this personal revelation which our leaders have been teaching us about for years. The Prophet and Twelve Apostles lead this, the Lord's Church, by this method, and I honor and follow them. As we become more in tune with the Spirit and build this spirituality into our lives, through this means we can help flood the land with faith in Jesus Christ. We are the generation which shall learn to bind Satan, for we will listen to him no more in our hearts.

This is my humble and sacred prayer, in the name of Jesus Christ, Amen.

Carolyn Pearce Ringger
Faith Unpuzzled Author

Appendix 1

Carolyn P. Ringger

Lesson 1/Puzzle Piece #1

Question: How does Faith work?

I. Our Goal Is To Find Out How Faith Works
  A. Discover what we are.
    1. We are "Intelligence"
    2. Intelligences can Think.
       a) Do you notice how your spirit-intelligence is always thinking inside your body?
    3. To think takes Mental Effort.
    4. "Faith Works by Mental Effort."
       a) Found in Lectures on Faith, by Joseph Smith, p. 61 #
    5. As Spirit Intelligence you will be with yourself for Eternity.
       a) Quotes on subject from Dr. Raymond Moody's book, Life After Life, p. 91 and Dr. George Ritchie's book, Return from Tomorrow, p. 47-78.
    6. Understanding Our Brain and How to Use It.
       a) Your Brain is a Servant Used by Your Intelligence through Thoughts
       b) Graph showing brain wave pattern.
  B. How Do You Grow In Faith
    1. Thoughts are an extension of our Faith.
       a) Positive Thought is Positive Faith.
       b) Negative Thought is Negative Faith.
    2. As a Man Thinketh In His HEART (or Thoughts - Feelings), So Is He. –Proverbs 23:7
       a) Do you think with your Heart in your chest or with your Heart in your mind?
  C. Unpuzzle the Word Heart

1. I Will Tell You In Your Mind and In Your Heart –
D&C 8:2-4

2. The Thoughts I Shall Put Into Your hearts – D&C
100:5

3. Prepare Your Minds and Hearts (Feelings) – Alma
16:16

D. Opposition In All Things Reveals That A Similar
System Is Controlled by Satan

    1. Satan Hath put It Into Their Hearts (Feelings) –
D&C 10:10, 13

    2. Chart: We Are Live Receiving Sets

II. How You May Distinguish Between the Two Internet
Servers:

A. Every Good Gift Cometh From Above –James 1:17 –
Moroni 7:12

B. Our Heavenly Father will never tempt us.

    1. Let No Man Say, I Am Tempted of God – James
1:12-14

III. The Devil Works By Putting Negative, Doubting, Evil,
Fearful and Judgmental Thoughts Into Our Mind.

A. The word devil in Hebrew means SPOILER. Bible
dictionary pg.656.

IV. Assignments

    1. Watch over your thoughts and words. Then replace
each Negative thought with a new Positive thought or
words.

    2. Look up the word Devil in the LDS version of the
Bible Dictionary p. 656, term SPOILER defined.

    3. Read book Return From Tomorrow, by Dr. George

Ritchie

4. Purchase CD by Dr. Charles Beckert, What Husbands Wish Their Wives Knew About Men, and A " Personal Search for the meaning of the Atonement" CD by Dr. W. Cleon Skousen.

Carolyn P. Ringger

Lesson 2/Puzzle Piece #2

Question: What Are My Hopes, Desires or Goals?

I. How do I use my Positive Mental Effort to make FAITH work for me?
  A. You must have hope –Moroni 7:1, 20-22, 25, and 40
    1. Next, read –Hebrews 11:1
    2. To Hope Takes Mental Effort
      a) Discuss –Hope for things you do not see.
  B. Let us say, Faith means to "Think" Positive Thoughts about your "HOPES"
  C. Ask in Faith, Nothing Wavering
    1. Read what James 1:5-8 says on this
    2. You must ask God in faith, nothing wavering... God works by the Law of Faith, with your Positive Thoughts
    3. Be not DOUBLE-MINDED
    4. Ask...What does it take to stop Negative, Doubting, Evil or Fearful Thoughts?
    5. Use Self-Talk and say:
    6. "I Erase or Delete the negative thought"
    7. Now Replace your Negative Thoughts with Positive Thoughts and Hopes.
    8. Agree Technique with thine adversary quickly (or your negative thoughts) See Matt. 5:25, 3 Nephi 12:25, then delete or cast out the evil thoughts.
    9. Did you know, that the male system is triggered visually? No wonder all souls need to dress modestly. Pornography is not a freedom of the press or Internet. It is a matter of triggering our sons and fathers to struggle more due to their male passion. Male stimulation has been referred to as being hardwired or automatic.

II. Ask for Light and Knowledge
  A. Make a LIST of your Hopes, and Desires – read them
    every morning and every night to plant them into your
    subconscious mind
  B. Parable of widow and unjust judge ... you are to weary
    the Lord Read Luke 18:1-8. Read also Ether chapters 2-
    3.
  C. Ask and Doubt Not – Read Mark 11:24
  D. Faith will be tried. – Read Ether 12:6

III. Assignments
    1. Watch over your thoughts and mentally delete all
    negative thoughts with your Self-Talk.
    2. Ask for Light and Knowledge to learn HOW the
    LAW OF FAITH works.
    3. Keep highlighting key words in the scriptures: Faith,
    Hope, Desire, Heart, Thoughts, Mind, Belief, Unbelief,
    Ask, Pray, The Eye of Faith, etc.
    4. Present your DESIRES to the Lord in Prayer and as a
    prayer in the HEART all day. Remember that the Lord
    is expecting you to voice your desires to Him before He
    can answer them.
    5. Read all of Moroni 7, Heb. 11, Ether 2-4 & 12, James
    1-5, Mormon 9.

Lesson 3/Puzzle Piece #3

Ask, Seek, Knock

Question: How can you get the Lord to help you achieve your Hopes and Desires?

I. Ask, Seek, Knock
  A. Joseph Smith said, "Weary the lord until He blesses you."
  B. Ask, seek, Knock – Christ told his followers (Matt. 7:7-11)
  C. "Ask the Lord – and He will Instruct You: - Example given by Theodore M. Burton
  D. Parable of Unjust Judge – Luke 18:1-8

II. Overcoming The World or Wickedness
  A. Rend the Veil of Unbelief – Ether 4"15-16
  B. Born of God overcometh the World – 1 John 5:4
  C. Become of One Heart and One mind
    1. Individually and unitedly through our righteous desires
    2. Fight pornography in movies, TV, magazines, etc.
    3. Prepare our "Saturday's Warriors"
    4. Fulfill our commitments as parents
    5. Overcome the Spoiler – he whispers into our ear
    6. Constant vigilance to deal with negative or evil thoughts

III. Repentance and forgiveness – Erase and Replace
  A. Process of repentance

B. Forgiveness of self and others in order to free ourselves
C. "I Erase and Replace" Script

IV. Assignment:
    1. Begin your own library of self help books and tapes. The materials teach you How to be self-reliant. You are to seek the Spirit Of The Lord to teach you as you follow the Lord's Prophet and leaders.

Lesson 4/Puzzle Piece #4

Nothing Wavering – No Doubting Thoughts

Question: Do I receive what I am asking for?
What is being Double-Minded?

I. Being double-minded – What does it mean? A definition.
 A. Chart – You Are A Mental Gardener

II. Thought Is Electrical Energy–Like Attracts Like
 A. Paul Dunn's Challenge: Write Your Diary in advance
 B. The Brain is a Servo-Mechanism
 C. Thought is Electrical energy
 D. Our Visualized thought is Translated into Reality

III. Are You Mentally Staying Single-Minded?
 A. Keep thoughts single to the glory of God
 B. Double-Mindedness can stop inspiration
 C. You command your thoughts
 D. To receive you must doubt not
 E. Parable of the mustard seed
 F. Your electromagnetic force field helps desires become reality.
 G. Plant right thoughts to harvest best

IV. You have free agency. You must doubt not.
 A. Doubting stops you from receiving hidden knowledge
 B. Scriptural quotes;
  1. Ye receive not because ye ask amiss – James 4:3, 7-8
  2. But their minds were blinded – 2 Cor. 3:14-16; 2

Cor. 4:3-4, 6

3. Have Ye Inquired of the Lord? – 1 Nephi 15:11

4. No mighty works because of unbelief – Matt. 13:58

5. Knowledge hidden because of unbelief – Ether 4:13-16

6. He whispereth in their ear – 2 Nephi 28:20, 22

7. Satan bound, hath no power – D&C 45:55; 1 Nephi 22:26

8. Believe and it shall be granted – Mormon 9:18-21

C. As A Man Thinketh

1. Lost books of the Bible speak of doubting thoughts stopping our desires

a) Remove from thee all doubting – 2 Hermas 9:1-11

D. Evil spirit can whisper in ear – missionary experience

Lesson 5/Puzzle Piece #5

Spiritual Communication
Listening to the Spirit

Questions: How does God speak to you? How do you hear it? What should you do about it? How does the spoiler speak to you?

I. Spiritual communication with God
  A. War in heaven between Michael and the Dragon – Rev.12:7–9.
  B. Let us prove them here with – chart and Scripture
  C. I stand at the door and knock –Rev. 3:20
  D. Receiving and recognizing personal revelation
    1. Quote from Pres. Kimball, – this voice more often felt than heard
    2. Quote from S. Dilworth Young – Spirit speaks Thoughts into our Mind
    3. Enlightened by the Spirit of truth –D&C 8:20–4
    4. Recognizing Personal Revelation
  E. Proof All Things, Hold Fast That which Is Good – Thess 5:21.
    1. We will prove them herewith – Abraham 3:25.
    2. Other Scriptures: D&C 98:14; Deut. 13:3
  F. You Are A Live Receiving Set – Chart
    1. The Voice of The Lord Came Into My Mind – Enos 1:10
    2. Above Voice of The Spirit – 1 Nephi 4:10–11; D&C 75:1

3. Still Small Voice Which Whisper of Through – D&C 85:6

G. How Do You Communicate with The Lord? – Mosiah 24:12

H. Study It Out then ask If right – D&C 9:7–9; Ether 3:1–6

I. Life Restored Through Inspiration of The Spirit – Missionary Experience

J. Faith – Joy Cycle

II. How Satan "The Spoiler" Works – Definition of word "Devil"

A. How Does the Spoiler Speak to You – always tries to Blair in your ears

1. A Spirit Can speak to Your Spirit – Most Often in Your Tone of Voice

B. You must Discern; Scriptural Quotes

1. Eracing Negative Thought Takes Mental Effort – James 4:7–8

2. He Whispereth In There Ears – 2 Nephi 28:22

3. Lying Sent Forth by Satan – 3 Nephi 1:22

4. Hard in There Hearts – 3 Nephi 2:1–2

5. Satan Hath Put It Into Their Hearts – D&C 10:10, 13–14, 20, 32

C. Lucifer tries to Hinder Temple Work – Quote from Church News

III. Spiritual Communication – Overview and Summary

A. You Are Accountable for Your Thoughts

B. Did I Not Speak Thoughts Into Your Mind? – D&C 6:23

IV. Assignments: Study, Ponder and Pray for Light and Knowledge to understand.

Carolyn P. Ringger

Lesson 6/Puzzle Piece #6

How To Make a Miracle

Questions: What Is A Miracle? How Do You Make A Miracle?

I. How Do You Bring About A Miracle?
  A. Faith precedes the Miracle. –Ether 12:12
  B. What precedes Faith?
    1. Your Hopes or Desires
    2. If ye have no hope ye must needs be in despair. – Moroni 10:22

II. Faith is what creates all Miracles and greatness in our lives.
  A. Without faith it is impossible to please God –Hebrews 11:6
  B. The Lord is waiting and wants to help us. –Mormon 9:21
  C. Formula for Faith –Believe, Doubt Not, Positive Inner Self-Talk

III. How Do You Make Miracles Happen in Your Life?
  A. Scriptural Examples:
    1. Alma and the Sons of Mosiah –Mosiah Ch. 27-29, Alma Ch. 14-26
    2. The 2,000 Stripling Young Warriors –Alma Chapters 53 and 56-58
    3. Lack of Faith – Fears in Your Heart –D&C 67:1-3, Mormon 9:21
  B. How miracles Will Come

1. Through Your "Spiritual Internet System"
2. Through Control of Your Thoughts
    a) Thought Produces Effects – Formula Given Us By God
3. Faith is an Ever Increasing Spiral
C. Faith and Miracles Today
    1. Missionary Miracles
        a) Sisters Morgan and Johnson In Mesa – Faith and Baptisms
        b) Two Sister Missionaries in North Germany Increase in Faith
D. Elders in Arizona Tempe Mission – Use their Faith
    1. More Miracles to Help Families – Story Examples
        a) Mike and Lorrie Anne Jones
        b) I Found an Answer to My Prayer – A Battle with Evil Thoughts
        c) Cultivate Quality of Faith – Excerpts of Letters
        d) A Letter from Globe, Arizona – A Visit of Peace
        e) Elder Steven Bush

IV. Assignments:
    1. Study the materials, ponder and pray for Light and Knowledge on how the Laws of Faith work. You will receive due to your faith.
    2. Mark your scriptures by Highlighting the faith wording.

Lesson 7/Puzzle Piece #7

The Faith – Joy Cycle

Question: How do you experience the Faith-Joy Cycle?

I. Review and Preview of the Faith Joy Cycle – It begins with your thoughts
   A. Think positive thoughts – build faith, miracles, joy.
   B. Think negative thoughts – experience depression, despair
   C. Thoughts can create emotions, which create actions

II. Chart Shows Faith-Joy Cycle and Depression Cycle, with scriptures

III. Taking the Shield of Faith – Scripture – D&C 27:17

IV. Ask the Lord and Get His approval – Scripture – Ether 2:23, 25

V. The Ten Steps of Faith – to Find Joy
   A. Ten basic steps
      1. Think of a problem you need to solve.
      2. Think about how you desire to solve it.
      3. Request for Light and Knowledge on the subject.
      4. Ponder over positive ideas, choose one, present it to the Lord to confirm.
      5. You will receive an answer.
      6. Do as the Spirit instructs.
      7. Your faith will be tried with Negative thoughts and

situations.

8. Ask, Doubt not, Weary the Lord until you receive for your confirmed desire is on its way.

9. Your Confirmed Righteous Desire is present = A Miracle

10. Give THANKS and Feel JOY!

VI. We are not a human being having spiritual experiences; we are a spiritual being having emotional, human experiences.

    A. Earth life is your school to learn self-control and to learn that through faith in Jesus Christ, all things are possible.

    B. Through your thoughts you can become pure in heart – and able to receive Beings Of Purity.

    C. Awaken, Ye Sleeping Giants – Remember, Men are that they might have JOY

Lesson 8 Puzzle Piece#8

Zion Is In The Heart

Question: How can you use this material to prepare for the Millennium?

I. The Millennium is Zion – Zion is the Pure in Heart
  A. Scriptures – Let Zion Rejoice, For Zion Is the Pure In Heart –D&C 97:21, 101:17–18
  B. How do you use this material to prepare for the Millennium?
    1. Quote – Our Best Defense – Bruce R. McConkie
  C. And Satan Shall Be Bound
    1. Scriptural quotes regarding the Millennium:
      a) 1 Nephi 22:26
      b) D&C 45:55
      c) D&C 43:31–32
      d) D&C 63:50–51
      e) D&C 101:29-31
    2. We are the generation that must learn to bind Satan because we listen to him no more.
    3. How may we prepare? By preparing our thoughts.
  D. Zion is the Pure In Heart.
  E. The Pure in Heart Shall See God –Matt. 5:8

II. How Will Satan Be Bound? – Institute Student Manual Quoted
  A. Because of the righteousness of his people – 1 Nephi 22:25
  B. Satan may not attempt any man – Joseph Fielding Smith quotes – D&C101:28

1. Two important reasons why Satan cannot temp mankind:
   a) Telestial wickedness will be destroyed
   b) The Lord will pour out his powers so Satan can't influence Saints
2. Both the power of God and Righteousness of the Saints necessary

C. Our Goal – To Become Your In Heart and Learn How We Can Make The Laws of Faith Work

III. The Scriptures Tell Own Story – Putting Scriptures together to assemble puzzle pieces.

Lesson 9/Puzzle Piece #9

You + Your Testimony

I. You + Your Testimony of Jesus Christ are the Missing Puzzle Piece

  A. You are One of the MOST Important People You Will Ever Know

  B. We are begotten sons and daughters unto God.

    1. Scriptural references

      a) Psalms 82:6

      b) Hosea 1:10

      c) D&C 76:24

  C. By Faith In Jesus Christ Miracles Are Wrought

  D. Moroni 7:36-37

  E. Things revealed to him who has faith In Jesus Christ -- Alma 26:22

  F. Your faith (in Jesus Christ) overcomes the world -- 1 John 5:4

    1. Your challenge – to overcome by faith.

    2. Awaken Ye Sleeping Giants – Awaken our dormant power of FAITH in Jesus Christ whereby ye may fulfill all things.

Carolyn P. Ringger

Appendix 2

The following is demonstrates the subtle way The Enemy is trying to destroy this great land.

"RULES FOR REVOLUTION"

Communist/socialist/progressive ways of understanding and overthrowing the government.

"Rules for Revolution"

ON A DARK NIGHT IN MAY, 1919, two lorries rumbled across a bridge and on to the town of Dusseldorf. Among the dozen rowdy, singing "Tommies" apparently headed for a gay evening were two representatives of the Allied military intelligence. These men had traced a wave of indiscipline, mutiny, and murder among the troops to the local headquarters of a revolutionary organization established in the town.

Pretending to be drunk, they brushed by the sentries and arrested the ringleaders--a group of thirteen men and women seated at a long table.

In the course of the raid the Allied officers emptied the contents of the safe. One of the documents found in it contained a specific outline of "Rules for Bringing About a Revolution." It is reprinted here to show the strategy of materialistic revolution, and how personal attitudes and habits of living affect the affairs of nations:

1) Corrupt the young. Get them away from religion. Get
them interested in sex. Make them superficial, destroy
their ruggedness.
2) Get control of all means of publicity and thereby:
a) Get people's minds off their government by focusing
their attention on athletics, sexy books and plays, and
other trivialities.
b) Divide the people into hostile groups by constantly
harping on controversial matters of no importance.
c) Destroy the people's faith in their natural leaders by
holding these latter [leaders] up to ridicule, obloquy,
and contempt.
d) Always preach true democracy, but seize power as fast
and as ruthlessly as possible.
e) By encouraging government extravagance, destroy its
credit, produce fear of inflation with rising prices and
general discontent.
f) Foment unnecessary strikes in vital industries,
encourage civil disorders and foster a lenient and soft
attitude on the part of government toward such
disorders.
g) By specious arguments cause the breakdown of the old
moral virtues; honesty, sobriety, continence, faith in
the pledged word, ruggedness.
3) Cause the registration of all firearms on some pretext,
with a view of confiscating them and leaving the
population helpless."--From New World News, Feb.
1946.

Perhaps we are not dedicated to the preservation
of this great land as we should be.

<u>N</u>otes

Carolyn P. Ringger

Made in the USA
Middletown, DE
13 July 2021